THE FINE PRINT

THE FINE PRINT

Between the Lines of Parenting, Children, and Relationship-Building

STACY CARY-THOMPSON, MD

Foreword By Hythia M. Phifer, MA, CMHC

THE FINE PRINT
Copyright © 2023 Stacy Cary-Thompson
All rights reserved.

Published by Publish Your Gift®
An imprint of Purposely Created Publishing Group, LLC

Unless otherwise indicated, scripture quotations are from the Holy Bible, King James Version. All rights reserved.

Scriptures marked NKJV are taken from the New King James Version®. Copyright © 1982 by Thomas Nelson. All rights reserved.

Printed in the United States of America

ISBN: 978-1-64484-495-3 (print)
ISBN: 978-1-64484-496-0 (ebook)

"Because you see the good in me, I know it's there."
—Unknown

DEDICATION

I come as one, but I stand upon the shoulders of many.

For my village—Some of you are still here with me in the physical form, and some of you are now among the ancestors. But all of you have been integral to my development and growth, to the adult I have become, and to the person I continue to show up as. You have nurtured me, taught me (formally and informally), loved me, shielded me, guided me, supported me, prayed for me, prayed with me, and acted on my behalf in ways that I don't even know. And you continue to show up.
THANK YOU.

To my Little Cherub—Mommy loves you so very much. It is my heart's joy to offer you my unconditional love. You are effortlessly precious and profound. I want you to know that it matters not what fills the rest of my days; each day, know that I can say with absolute certainty that you are the best thing I have ever known. Elijah, you are evidence that God loves me immensely.

To Little Cherub's village—Know that I cherish you.
THANK YOU.

To Nugget—Mommy is so excited to meet you! I love you already, and I thank God for the miracle you are.

To my Hubby—Thank you for the way that you express your love for me. It nourishes me. With you, support is a verb, and for that I thank you Baby. You are my person. Your partnership has made the roughest journeys bearable. Your patience has been invaluable. Our laughter together has been a source of contentment. I feel blessed to journey the rest of my life with you. I love you always, sweetie.

To Mommy—For your unwavering support, for all you have given, and for all you are—I love you. For teaching me how to love and how to give—thank you. I have always admired you. I appreciate you even more now that I'm a mommy myself. You are such a beautiful human being, and it is the ultimate blessing to have you as my mother. Thank you.

To Sissy—My cheerleader, my favorite Taboo partner, the sharer of most of my inside jokes. I love you and our bond. Through your example (even when we were kids), you gave me permission to love my mind, and I thank you. I thank you also for being an example of someone with a solid sense of self. I've always been watching.

To the Thompson & Dickerson Tribe—I am so grateful for the way that you have always embraced me, and I feel lucky to have gained not just a wonderful husband, but a wonderful family in you. I love you all.

Dedication

To my Bahamian family—I love you.

For Daddy—I wish that I could thank you for all the things that I was oblivious to that have now come into my awareness as a parent. And I wish I could apologize for the gray hairs I caused. I wish that I could share this accomplishment with you. I wish that I could laugh with you again. I wish a lot of things, so many things. I miss you. But through the ache, my heart smiles warmly at your memory. My love for you transcends space and time. Thank you, Daddy.

To those I call Friend—Know that I think you're dope! Know that I deeply appreciate the ways in which we laugh, support, confide in, protect, learn from, make space for, turn up with, show out for, enrich, pray for, see, and uplift each other. All of that. What a blessing it is to have good friends!

To God—For it all, all of it, I thank you. The glory is Yours.

TABLE OF CONTENTS

FOREWORD

by Hythia M. Phifer, MA, CMHC

Last spring, I was child-sitting for my ten-year-old nephew who was staying over at my house on a school night. Now, this was at the dawn of the COVID-19 pandemic. Fear, confusion, and apprehension for the days ahead plagued the minds of many households, including my own. We were all really scared!

Additionally, one of my parents was dealing with a serious health-related struggle, and I was trying my best to manage my heart and mind in the midst of so much uncertainty.

On this fateful morning, as the nation was waiting, fretfully, for more information about the dreaded, novel COVID-19, I was having a communication breakdown with my nephew over morning chores. This particular breakdown followed an almost sleepless night filled with wails and yowls from my boisterous cat, Osiris. Needless to say, I was in a vile mood. So, when my nephew asked if he really had to clean the litter box and the bits of litter that had fallen onto the floor, I answered him with a stern look, a stern voice, and stern words that probably went something like, "Do not make me ask you again."

Sometime later, I was contemplating what had taken place between my nephew and myself. Perhaps the intention of his question was clarification rather than challenge.

Perhaps the sluggishness of his behavior was warranted considering our shared experience of an untimely feline serenade a few hours prior. Perhaps his resistance to his chores was valid given the disoriented state of our entire livelihood.

As with many instances where I am faced with a child-proximate dilemma, I phoned my decades-long friend, Dr. Stacy, whose pediatrics certification had navigated me through many a stormy sea. When you have a doctor as a friend, you tend to lean on them for a variety of issues—medical, emotional, spiritual, and otherwise. I told her what had occurred between my nephew and me, and like a good friend she listened actively, asked clarifying questions, and offered affirmational verbal cues.

When I'd completed my account, as if by magic, I'd realized that my surliness, valid though it was, had nothing to do with my nephew. Through reflective listening and thoughtful questioning, Stacy was able to help me turn my outward gaze inward, toward my own thoughts, feelings, and experiences; toward my own perspectives, priorities and behaviors; and toward my truth: I really wanted my nephew to feel secure in the troubling times and I had no idea how to help him with that, especially when I was being impacted by similar troubles. Together, Stacy and I developed a plan for me to explain to my nephew that he was not the cause or the container for my emotional experience; and that he was precious to me, no matter what I was feeling.

This is the power of conversations with Stacy:

1. Reflective listening, questioning, and coaching
2. Compassionate validation and ongoing encouragement
3. Expert advice from a skilled professional who is also a lifelong learner

A healthy dose of each of these powerful supports is packed into the following pages.

As a clinical mental health counselor with a specialization in trauma and expressive arts therapy, I have experience working with children across the developmental spectrum. From engaging children in play therapy during after-school programming to developing goals that increase adolescent stabilization in a residential setting, I have been responsible for the healthy adjustment and well-being of countless children and their supportive networks. I have also met a variety of children and adults who have felt anger, frustration, and bafflement in their relationships with one another.

Often the source of the rupture in child-adult relationships lies within the perspectives of the adult. That is not to say that adults are the problem of every child-adult relationship. Children are people too, and all people have patterns of behavior that dictate how we respond or react to each and every situation. However, it *is* true that children, from infancy to adolescence, are learning a variety of perspectives and patterns of behavior *right before our very eyes.* How we interact with them is teaching them how to act, whether we know it or not, whether we mean to or not.

Children learn from what we teach them intentionally and unintentionally, from what we say and do and show. And while we, adults, are imperfect beings who are still learning from our successes and our growth edges, we hold a great deal of power over the impact we have on the lives of children around us. And if you'll permit me to quote Peter Parker's wise Uncle Ben, "With great power comes great responsibility."

Within the following pages, Stacy emphasizes that our "perspectives influence our priorities [...] and [our] priorities influence [our] behaviors." So, we must *be intentional* in order to give the very best of ourselves to the children we raise, neighbor, supervise, coach, mentor, and nurture.

I have been privileged to witness Stacy's parenting *and* pediatric acumen, which is enhanced by innate clinical abilities including a therapeutic disposition and a bedside manner that is warm and natural. I've witnessed, firsthand, her ability to operationalize her knowledge of various interventions, shifting and tailoring strategies to the unique needs of every child. And, perhaps most significant to me as a therapist, I've witnessed how she prioritizes the socio-emotional experience of the children and families she serves, adapting formalized training and empathic intuition to support the entire well-being of those under her care.

She is a true scientist, a researcher, and a perpetual scholar. Her ability to integrate and implement new information sets her apart from many professionals who claim expertise. She is devoted to increasing her knowledge and awareness and polishing her skills.

She is thoughtful and considerate, weighing the intention and impact of every behavior and action. She is planful, thorough, and committed to every undertaking. In the following narrative, she is vulnerable, sharing the wisdom she has gained through the *opportunity of her challenges.* She embodies intentionality in every aspect of her life, every domain of her existence.

Many of the effective strategies she has cultivated are present within this text, shared with casual flair as though she is speaking with a friend, because that's Stacy. A coach and a friend who walks with you, learning alongside you and encouraging you on the journey.

I commend you, dear reader, for choosing to embark on this journey. Know that you are part of a constellation of folks who are passionate about children, their growth, and their futures. This kind of compassion cannot be taught, which makes you an invaluable resource and a precious member of our community. Welcome! My hope is that you are able to witness and celebrate your own growth, enjoy the fruits of your endeavors, and share your bounty with all the blessed people in your care. Thank you for adding your presence to this vital and vibrant fellowship!

Happy reading,
Hythia Phifer, Master in Mental Health Counseling

Hythia Phifer is a clinical mental health counselor and clinical consultant with a specialty in trauma-informed interventions and expressive arts therapy. She is also a writer, a performance artist, a lover of anime, and an avid reader. Currently, she is providing clinical consultation for the Boston Public Health Commission's Capacity Building and Training Initiative (CBTI).

PREFACE

As a pediatrician, I am an expert in child development. And from where I sit, I also get to observe the entire life cycle. I'm in the delivery room or operating room at birth; I witness the stages of development—infancy, early childhood, middle childhood, adolescence, young adulthood. I see families as they age, and I watch the family dynamic across generations. I consider myself fortunate in this way.

Pediatrics is different from other fields of medicine because there is the triadic relationship of patient-parent-physician, which adds complexity. It means considering the child's best interests as well as what his or her parents see as the family's best interests. I love pediatrics because babies and young people have this way of causing your positive elements of humanity to spring forth. Your layers fall away. *That's* why I'm a pediatrician. Because I like who I am in that element, my help and my giving in that space are always from a place of purpose and contentment.

Many people think pediatrics is a world filled with rainbows and stickers and unicorns. While there is no shortage of cuteness, and there are many, many joys in the world of pediatrics, it is also an arena where you will see the ugliness of humanity. The dark side of pediatrics includes dealing with things like child maltreatment—including physical abuse, sexual abuse, factitious illness (medical child abuse), neglect, trafficking, verbal abuse, and psychological/emotional abuse. I have no tolerance for these things. When you've witnessed a sexual assault exam performed on a two-year-old child, or when you've admitted a child to the intensive care unit (ICU) with a liver laceration and bladder contusion because they were beaten by mom's boyfriend, you develop a bit of cynicism. So yes, I have seen evil. I know that there are some miserable people out there that are hungry for the suffering of others. But in large part, I know that most parents really are not trying to harm their children. Most parents are out here doing the best they can. I see you. Ultimately, parents want what is best for their child and a strong parent-child relationship can help lead to better outcomes for children. I stand with you.

Intriguingly enough, approximately 25 percent of all pediatric office visits are associated with children's social or behavioral problems. So it is not at all uncommon for parents to seek assistance from pediatricians in raising socially-integrated, well-adjusted children, in addition to treating childhood illness. As such, I have a greater understanding of how successful families function, and of how to teach other families to be more supportive. So when I talk about parenting, I can tell you that I have lived the experiences—personally, with my patients, and with my coaching clients.

Yet, I do not approach this from a place of perfection at all! Even with my expertise, I have the same concerns that I think all parents have. I don't know how my kid will turn out! There are so many independent variables. But I can control my attitude, my actions, and my effort. So while you can always hope that things turn out for the best, you can also choose to be intentional. It takes intention to parent the child you have and not the child you were or who you wish they would be. It is my goal to help parents understand how they can be more intentional. There is power in intention. It is my goal to help parents grow with their children through various stages of development, and through situations both ordinary and extraordinary. It is my hope to give parents the courage to change narratives that need to change. It is my hope for them to feel seen. It is my hope for them to feel empowered to connect with their children's gifts, potential, and importance to this world. It is my hope for children to be safe, healthy, happy, heard, and whole.

INTRODUCTION

Books change the way information and traditions are passed along. Instead of the one-to-one experience I'm used to in the exam room with a patient, I can leverage my impact and it can be one-to-thousands with a book. One of the many reasons that I am passionate about my clinical practice, as well as my parent coaching, is because I cherish the perspective that it affords me. One thing I know as an enduring truth is that being in relationship can cloud our judgement, and it can escape our grasp to be able to see things in their entirety and to call things as we see them. I have learned this time and time again, both through my patients and through my coaching clients. For that reason, I deeply cherish the perspective I am able to have from my positioning. Through that, I like to build bridges and make connections, and I want others to tap into their power to do so. Because I am extremely passionate about children's wellbeing, it made sense to write this book. It's about being able to go into your cabinet and have the tools to give children their best life. Ultimately, it is my hope to *transform lives for generations.*

Beyond my passion for children's well-being, I wrote this book for several reasons. By sharing a thoughtful approach to child-rearing, we can create more positive parent-child relationships. I believe that healthy children become healthy adults. Because I was blessed to experience a rich, loving home growing up, I want as many children as possible to experience that as well. Through my practice, I have come to consider the entirety of each child's being. So when I see a child, I see a human being, a mind, a spirit, and a soul in development. Oftentimes, I interpret my world and interactions through the lens of child wellness, and I am passionate about it because I recognize that so much of a person's childhood is shaped by other people's choices.

As a neuroscientist, I am enthralled by the structure and function of the brain and nervous system—how it develops, matures, and maintains itself. Yet, I am also particularly fascinated by its impact on behavior and cognitive function, as you'll get a taste of throughout this book. As a pediatrician, I view my role as being a partner with parents in making sure children are safe and healthy. I also look at myself as a child advocate—someone who empathizes with and amplifies the voice and perspective of children. And I marvel at children's capacity to learn, to rebound, to persist, and to forgive. Observing children and their families, and through all of my experiences, I have learned so much and feel it incumbent upon me to share the philosophies that I have come to know that drive much of the advice I am able to provide.

I am also a strong believer in the village mindset. Our needs as defined by evolution are for community, contact, collaboration, and connection. As such, I wholeheartedly believe that it takes a village to raise a child. Furthermore, no one relationship can meet all of our needs, and similarly, no parent can meet all of their child's needs. This is where the village comes in. We're better together as human beings. We're better in connection. We're better when we have the benefit of each other's perspectives. We're better when we help each other see what we can't see for ourselves.

Your village can be comprised of many players, and their level of importance to you—as well as their level of involvement with your child—will often shift over the course of your child's upbringing. In the words of author Bruce Feiler, "You can't have too many adults who love your kid." So I look at this book as an expression of love, and as a way for me to offer an *extended village* along your parenthood journey.

Who This Book Is NOT For

This book is not for someone unwilling to break out of old habits. This is not for someone unwilling to entertain new ways of thinking. This is not for someone who believes that their way is the "right way" simply because they are older. This is not for someone who is disinterested in self-reflection. Nor is this book for someone who believes there is no value in their child's voice and perspective.

Who This Book IS For

This book is for parents—whether you're new at it or have lots of skin in the game. This book is for separated co-parents seeking better alignment of their ideals in order to more harmoniously create the environment they envision for their child. It is also for *parent-proxies*. Now wait a minute, what are parent-proxies? Parent-proxies can represent child caregivers in a nontraditional household. Or for instance, it can also represent an involved, cool auntie that simply wants to better understand the kids she adores in order to maximize the quality of their time together when they hang out. Parent-proxies are those members of the village that neighbor, supervise, coach, mentor, nurture, and help us raise our children. So, parent-proxies, I acknowledge you. I see you.

This book is also for expectant parents. It is for families considering adoption. It is for grandparents that are primary caregivers. It is for grandparents seeking to do things differently with their grandbabies than they did with their own children. It is for educators, health professionals, or others in a profession that heavily engages with and influences children. It is for anyone who cares about children. Regardless of how your unique village looks, what I know is that invariably there are people who stand in the gap for primary providers because no parent can be with their child all the time, even though it's a 24/7 commitment. This book is also for anyone interested in examining their own childhood through a new lens.

I am not saying that what I have written here is gospel. But I do believe that my approaches to parenting are effective—across class and culture. Of course, there will be circumstances that fall outside of the recommendations contained in this book, but my goal is not to be right all the time. My goal is to provide a framework that allows you to operate in such a way so as to yield the greatest return. Children are our greatest investment. I am the expert in child development, health, and behavior. You are the expert on your child. Together, magic can happen!

I want to be deliberate in acknowledging that the COVID-19 pandemic has caused many of us to pivot. And in so doing, many parents are spending a lot more time with their kids. Despite the chaos of the outside world—during a global pandemic or not—I want kids and their parents to experience a healthy home.

My hope is to move people with my words. The takeaways from this book will be different for each individual, but in reading this book, you will learn practical as well as research-based strategies that can be applied in your everyday life. There will be tips you want to incorporate and make yours, and there will be tips you want to discard. You will laugh. You will think. You will feel seen. You will tap into your *phenomenal parenting power (P3)*!

Happy reading!
—Dr. Stacy

PART I:
THE BASICS

CHAPTER 1

GOALS

"I do my best because I'm counting on you counting on me."
—Maya Angelou

If I had to describe parenting, I would say that it is a beautiful, unglamorous, hilarious, heartbreaking, frustrating, challenging, exhausting, rewarding journey with a mix of monotony, at times agonizing self-accountability, and sprinkles of twists and turns. Parenting can be a lot of late nights and early mornings—and I don't mean the sexy kind! Parenting requires prioritization, juggling, and adaptability.

Becoming a parent forces you to view several things differently: yourself, your expectations of others, and what you allow. It is transformative. In the words of my friend and mom of three, Marcee, "Motherhood has created an awareness of disparaging messages I have internalized." I too can identify with how parenthood compels you to examine your relationship with yourself. For me, it has also been a journey of epiphanies. Once you become a parent, never again are you not a parent. Think about that. That is profound. And though a parent is a child's first teacher, I learn just as much, if not more, from my kid. I plan to teach him through the mistakes that I will invariably and actively make with him at my side, and I will teach him from the wisdom that I have acquired.

The parent-child relationship is one that nurtures the physical, emotional, and social development of the child. Ultimately, children first learn the language, the essence, and the energy of love from us parents, and that is something that permeates all aspects of life. Healthy parent involvement and intervention in the child's day-to-day life can help the child exhibit optimistic and confident social behaviors, and even lay the foundation for better academic skills. Furthermore, we know that children who have a healthy relationship with their parents are more likely to develop positive relationships with other people around them. This is because the parent-child relationship is the primary relationship of one's life. It is the relationship that provides the foundation upon which all other relationships are based and it determines the child's attachment style, personality, behavior, and life choices.

I don't think that anyone would dispute that parents are providers and protectors. But there is much more to parenting than being a provider of material necessities and wants. And when it comes to being protectors, that is a multifaceted task. Naturally, we want to protect our children from the cruel, unforgiving, unfair, prejudiced world. Yet we must also protect them from their curiosities when they are unable or unwilling to prevent their exposure to harm. For an example, think about stove knob covers. One day, I was making my kid a grilled cheese sandwich. To mitigate potential risk, and because I know my child, I put the pan on the back burner. He was standing at my hip, supervising my every move, anxiously waiting in anticipation for what was to him filet mignon. He would walk around the kitchen but always come back to my side, and he would occasionally attempt to fiddle with the stove knobs. Thankfully, there were covers on them. I use this simple example of my child as a toddler because he was behaving as I would expect a toddler to behave. Because I anticipated this, the stove knob covers were in place to protect him. He, like all typical toddlers, approached the world with a seemingly infinite curiosity and wonder. Did he want to burn himself? No. He just wanted to explore how the cool shiny circles jutting out from the stove worked. But there's another layer of protectiveness that many parents feel fiercely about: protecting their children from others. This includes, as age-appropriate, protecting them from the unfortunate ugly truths of the world. And sometimes, we must also protect them from ourselves. Let that simmer. Parenthood is provision, protection, and so much more.

In the words of Brené Brown, "If you're brave enough, often enough, you're going to fall." That in and of itself can be challenging to accept, but we swallow that pill of reality and smile at the rewards that lie on the other side of bravery. But also in that swallow is the feeling that, "I don't want to see you hurt," *and* the feeling that, "I hope I don't make you scared to try." Parenthood is tricky. It is as much what we do for our children as it is what we teach them to do for themselves. There is always at play a delicate balance of trying to figure out how to let your kids forge their own paths, and being there for them when they do fall.

Sometimes parenting is just caring that they fell and kissing the boo-boos. Sometimes it's giving a Band-Aid— literally or figuratively. Sometimes it's picking them up. Sometimes it's extending a hand. Sometimes it's coaching them through staying down long enough to not miss the lesson. Sometimes it's just being a watchful eye. Sometimes it means redirecting. Sometimes it's about encouraging. Sometimes it requires scolding. After all, kids need both gentleness and grit. Sometimes parenthood is just being. I am learning and growing in how to navigate my son's path every day. I don't know everything that my child needs to learn. He wasn't born with a syllabus. Therefore, I have to learn to accept the things I can't account for.

Besides teaching them their first words, how to tie their shoes, the difference between right and wrong, and how to ride their bikes, there are five things that parents are integral in influencing in their children:

1. Their internal dialogue

2. How to interact with the opposite sex (regardless of their sexual orientation)

3. Their relationship with food

4. Their relationship with money

5. What to tolerate from others

This will be expounded upon throughout the book.

Now, it is not uncommon for parents to have goals that they want their children to achieve. Parents work hard to ensure that their children are developing at the correct rate and don't "fall behind." But let's shift the focus. What do you hope to achieve as a parent? I think all parents should aspire to achieve goals for themselves in raising their children, so let's start by discussing what those goals may look like.

Develop Your Child's Conscience and Esteem

I must tell you. I attribute much of my success to my village. For all the times when I probably shouldn't have made it, I persisted and persevered because the belief that I could do it was louder than the "no's" inside of my head or outside of my circle. This is a notion I reflect on not infrequently. Because I know the potency of powerful messaging, I want my voice to be the loudest voice until my child finds his own. If you think about it, that's typically the way it is. Through my own parenthood journey, I have had front-row seats to the nuances of development. I've watched my baby go from babbling to speaking, literally because I gave him words to speak. In this same way, I too shape his thoughts. So until he develops his own thoughts and views, I want to share mine, and I want to make sure what I offer is solid. As a parent, you should provide your child with what will ultimately become their *positive* self-talk: their conscience, their esteem. Think about that. Eventually, they will be able to independently apply what they learned from you about themselves. Think about how much power you have. You shape their concept of self-worth. You become the voice in their head. Will it be something they can carry with them, or will it be something they need to overcome and heal from? What are you feeding them about themselves?

Shape What Your Child Is Attracted To

While the need for human connection is innate, the ability to form healthy, loving relationships is learned. Children learn from us not because we tell them what to do, but because they are constantly observing us and mimicking us and using our actions and words as guidelines for how they should speak and act. As a parent or parent-proxy, you influence your child's basic values. You also influence the communication patterns, conflict behaviors, and supportive behaviors that they develop, as well as those that they will seek familiarity with in others. Here, I would like to point out that "normal" and "normalized" are two different things. Something can be *normalized*, but very much unhealthy, futile, extreme, or unfit. For instance, this is partly why interparental conflict or intimate partner violence tends to show up in a cyclical way. At some point, those involved become accustomed to, and consciously or subconsciously attracted to, people and behaviors that feel familiar (even if toxic) because it was normalized. And what I know about human behavior is that we tend to allow people into our lives when we see something in them that we have a connection with. We can also seek connections with people that allow us to fulfill roles that are familiar, even if those roles no longer serve us. So, parents and parent-proxies must wield their power wisely.

Nurture Your Child's Gifts and Talents

There's a bay window in my living room, and my son likes to climb onto the large windowsill, hide behind the curtains, then dramatically appear and start singing. I don't know what will become of this. Perhaps he'll be a performer or a record producer. Maybe he won't. But what I know currently is that he likes to sing, and he actually has a lovely voice and can carry a tune, so I encourage his interest in music. I sing with him (sometimes in unison, sometimes I harmonize). I attend his "concerts" and cheer (loudly); yes, I'm THAT mama. I expose him to a variety of musical stylings (including the oldies). I even exposed him to the piano. Well, it's actually a keyboard. It was gifted to him on his last birthday. I wanted him to have an instrument, besides his voice, that he could get acquainted with if he wanted. I wanted him to see the relationship notes have to one another. He seems to have a particular affinity for music, and I wanted to nurture that. So parents, whether it means enrolling them in gymnastics, buying them a paint set, attending a recital, sending them to basketball camp, or proudly wearing the first shirt they ever made for you, it is up to us to nurture their gifts, talents, and interests. We provide the encouragement, the means, and the environment for them to develop their potential.

Minimize Toxicity

We can't prevent every single potentially damaging thing, nor is it our job to shield our children from adversity. However, what we can do is ensure they don't feel alone in pain that comes their way and we can equip them with coping skills to deal with life's obstacles and their associated feelings. Also, we can do our best to be a part of their healing and recovery. A relatively simple notion, but certainly not an easy practice. Simple, not easy.

Mold a Decent Member of Society

The saying goes, "No man is an island entire of itself; every man is a piece of the continent, a part of the main [. . .]." John Donne may not have used the most inclusive pronouns, but his message is clear. None of us do this thing called life alone. We share this experience, so we must contribute to the betterment of the whole. We must be kind to others, treat them with dignity, be tolerant, be empathetic, possess moral fiber, and conduct ourselves with integrity—what I like to think of as *Sesame Street* fundamentals. (I'm a longtime ardent lover of *Sesame Street*, by the way!)

Teach Them to Think Critically

Critical thinking happens when children draw on their existing knowledge and experience, as well as their problem-solving skills, to do things like:

- Compare and contrast
- Explain why things happen
- Evaluate ideas and form opinions
- Understand the perspectives of others
- Predict what will happen in the future
- Think of creative solutions

Children need to learn to think critically if they are going to be successful in today's complex world. Teaching them critical thinking includes encouraging them to interrogate relationships and examine how they would like to participate in their relationships. Children should interrogate their own assumptions. Children should also learn to think critically about the messages they receive. Teaching skepticism is good—it can help kids determine what is safe or unsafe in the world. A healthy dose of skepticism can also make them less impulsive. However, it doesn't begin to stick until children hit age eight or nine. And it should be taught carefully. Too much skeptical thinking can lead to cynicism about the intent of others and the broad dismissal of facts, which tends to lead to poor decision-making. Another fear is that children will reach the wrong conclusions even though they have engaged in critical thinking. Well, of course they will! That is to be expected. Critical thinking requires practice. Mistakes are a way to fine-tune that practice so it eventually turns into a robust skepticism that welcomes any logical conclusion. So, how can parents and parent-proxies help kids without turning them into pessimists or dampening their creativity? As with many things, it is all about modeling the right behaviors, according to Dr. Shannon McHugh, a practicing clinical psychologist who focuses on working with children and families. I tend to agree.

Parents and parent-proxies that want to model skeptical behavior do the following:

- **They Ask Lots of Questions When Making Decisions in Front of Their Kids** When looking to buy a new television or piece of equipment in front of their kids, parents should make sure they are asking lots of questions and doing lots of research. "In regular situations in life, parents should ask questions before they make a decision," says McHugh. That is especially true if they are in front of their kids. If they're choosing between two televisions to replace an old, busted one, they can ask questions about the quality of the television, the price point, the payment plans, etc. After they've asked those questions and seem satisfied with the information they've received, they can make a decision. Doing so in front of their kids helps teach kids to interrogate the information and their own motivations.

- **They Explain the Decisions They Make to Kids** Parents should explain, when possible, the decisions they've made to their kids. Now I can imagine some contorted facial expressions, particularly if you're from a generation that mandates kids do what they are told, no questions asked, no explanations given. However, saying, "We're getting this TV" is less helpful than explaining why. This is also a way to get kids engaged in decision-making without necessarily asking them to participate in that process, which isn't always appropriate.

- **They Interrogate Kids About Their Own Decisions** Parents who want skeptical kids ask them why they do what they do. While kids aren't often deciding between two flat-screen televisions, they sometimes choose to wear certain shoes or a special T-shirt. Ask them why. Is it because they are more comfortable? Do they prefer a certain color? This encourages kids to consider why they might make decisions. This doesn't teach skepticism per se, but it does teach them about the ways in which they process information. It is an opportunity to demonstrate genuine curiosity about what makes them tick.

Prepare Them for Adulthood

As someone who used to be addicted to being busy, one of the things I struggled with was not giving my son a chance to practice buttoning his shirt. Because I was on-the-go and wanted to move fast, it was "easier" for me to just go ahead and do it. But I later learned that it might give him the message that he is incapable. So my concern shifted from one of efficiency to one of concern about the long-term costs to his sense of self. Full transparency, I was guilty of overhelping.

To paraphrase Julie Lythcott-Haims, author, speaker, and activist: When we over-help, over-protect, over-direct, and over-correct, we deprive our children of the chance to build self-efficacy, which is a fundamental tenet of the human psyche. Self-efficacy is built when one sees that one's own actions lead to outcome, not one's parent's actions on one's behalf, but when one's *own* actions lead to outcomes. So, for our kids to become successful adults, they have to do more of the thinking, planning, deciding, doing, hoping, dreaming, trial and error, and experiencing of life for themselves. Adulthood brings with it the ability to vote, drink alcohol, and rent a car; and let us not forget there's also the luxury of paying bills. But ultimately, being an adult is largely about becoming more comfortable with uncertainty and gaining the know-how to keep going. So as a parent, it is incumbent upon me to make sure that my child has the habits, the mindset, the skillset, and the wellness to be successful wherever they go.

If these goals seem desirable and reasonable to you, then keep reading. This book will help you frame your thoughts. Frame your thoughts, alter your approach. Alter your approach, receive different results. But you can still maintain your own special sauce because I wouldn't have it any other way.

CHAPTER 2

MINDSET

"If you are not willing to learn, no one can help you.
If you are determined to learn, no one can stop you."

—Zig Ziglar

In addition to treating patients (the kids) in my clinical practice, I created a space, *Cary Cares Parenting LLC*, to take on parents as clients in order to expand my reach. Through *Cary Cares*, a parent coaching program I developed, I provide an extended village, compassionate validation, longevity perspective, and a practical approach to the intricacies of parenting. Parents and parent-proxies learn to develop the skills and habits that allow them to more effectively manage situations both ordinary and extraordinary. The overarching mindset that fuels the transformation that takes place through *Cary Cares Parenting* is the belief that relationships are life's enduring rewards. Therefore, deliberate, intentional investment in how we show up is always worth the effort. At the start of *Cary Cares*, there are always several questions that I ask each person to ponder. I call these the Necessary Nine:

1. What is something you wish you could do differently as a parent?
2. How would you describe your parent(s)?
3. How do you think your child/children would describe you?
4. What is your favorite thing about your parent/ each of your parents?
5. What is your current relationship like with your parent(s)?
6. If your parent(s) died today, would you have regrets about the state of your relationship?
7. If your parent(s) is/are deceased, what was your relationship with them like before they died?
8. What is one thing you learned from your parents that you wish you could unlearn?
9. What is one thing that you are most appreciative that your parents taught you?

The answers to these questions are quite revealing about your parenting values and can inform you in some way about how you should navigate the relationship with your child and the work you need to do. We define our dialogue, and in a sense, our future, through the questions we choose to address. It is the dialogue and struggle with the question that carries the promise of a deeper resolution. When we are intentional about the relationships we cultivate with our children, we can transform lives for generations.

All of our relationships reveal things about us that we sometimes never knew were there. Relationships can show you the parts of yourself that you need to amplify, and the parts you need to have a funeral for. For parents engaged in self-improvement, that means their kids see a human person who is steadily more emotionally stable in adverse situations. But it also shows them that a strategy of self-improvement is one that pays off in relationships. Making the work you do on yourself apparent to your children helps in several ways. It normalizes seeking help. It builds a child's emotional vocabulary. It improves communication. It teaches resilience. And it promotes relationship-building skills.

Remember, you are the first change that needs to happen. Know also that anything inside of our awareness is something we can change. To be aware is to see a scenario playing out in front of you and know the familiar dynamics that are contributing. The other kind of awareness is to be aware of what you are feeling instead of choosing avoidance. I acknowledge that at times, the awareness can seem too uncomfortable to even contemplate; but the greater awareness we have of our tendencies and motivations, the more likely we are to overcome them so that we may then actively choose what we are motivated by.

During my time working with parents and parent-proxies, I pose a series of *phenomenal parenting power* questions (**P3Q's**).

You will be able to find a collection of these at the end of each section of this book. At the very least, they will cause you to be reflective in some key ways. At most, they will challenge ways in which you may be stuck in tradition and ego. Additionally, I encourage you to take a moment to ponder what love means to you. Once you have this definition in your mind, hold on to it and know that this kind of introspection is necessary. Also know that loving sometimes means getting out of your comfort zone. But, when your perspective changes, your approach changes.

CHAPTER 3

PERSPECTIVE AND PRIORITIES

"Diversity is the basic nature of the universe. If you are developing a relationship with someone else, there will be some differences. The key to successful relationships is the ability to deal with those differences."

—Anshu Shrivastava

I often say, "It's all a matter of perspective." We know more than our children when it comes to many things, except for their perspectives. That brings me to a hilariously fond memory of my dad. He once shared a story with my sister and I about "Shirley Goodness." His parents were a deacon and deaconess, so he grew up going to church frequently. He talked about how he would often wonder why everyone talked about "Shirley Goodness." Who was she? What did she do? Why was she so special? Well, there was a particular context in which he would usually hear about Miss Shirley. In the Bible, Psalms 23:6 (King James Version) states, "Surely goodness and mercy shall follow me all the days of my life: and I will dwell in the house of the Lord for ever." So when my dad got older, he finally realized that it wasn't "Shirley Goodness" that they were saying, but "surely goodness." Cue the belly laughs! Oh, how

Sissy and I just laughed and laughed! We were so amused. Hopefully that memory got a grin out of you too. I share that not only for levity, but to also demonstrate how, in my dad's childlike mind, the church folk were talking about a person. That was his perspective, and he was trying to make sense of it in his own way.

Kids help us to make sense of things too. I woke up one November morning surrounded by the crisp, cool air coming in through the crack in the window, just like I like it, with the comforter over my shoulders. My body was cozy, but my mind felt like it hadn't slept. Immediately upon waking, I felt heavy as I formulated my to-do list, filled with many residual tasks from days prior. I woke up feeling guilty, ashamed, and stressed. As I laid awake trying to get my mind together so I could seize the day, my five-year-old walked into the bedroom. His smile, with all of his cute little baby teeth, was easy and bright. His eyes warm and joyful. My gaze switched from distant to inviting. I am excited to see his sweet face, and for a moment, I escape the weight of all of my worries. In that moment, I look at him, and he is genuinely happy to see me. It is indeed a good morning. I am humbled. I thought, very simply, very matter-of-factly, "Wow, he loves me." In his eyes, I noticed no record of wrongdoing. In his face, I felt forgiveness. He didn't care about what did and didn't get checked off my to-do list the previous day. He was present. He was happy. He was happy for *today*. Being present, and being happy, seemed to be one and the same. And in that moment, I thought, "This is my lesson for today."

Clearly, children can bring an easy delight to situations, even without trying. But one of the many other things I love about kids is that there is always a certain honesty in their actions. Even when they lie or manipulate, as all children do at one point or another, that honesty is still there because they are true to what they need. One of the keys of parenting is understanding what they need, and how that message is packaged.

Youngsters can be relentless about getting their needs met. I actually admire that. At times, I even envy it. Yet one of the markers of maturity—and an expectation of adulting—is that you exercise the ability to set your needs aside at times. The incongruence is glaring. Grappling with the discordance between childhood and adulthood can be especially challenging while trying to meet your child's needs when your own needs aren't being met (more on this in Chapter 27 on Self-Care). Recognize that both you and your child interact with the world differently. If you are committed to accommodating those differences, even as those differences change over time, and if you are willing to maintain space and grace to consider their perspective, the result will never come up void. Perspective is constructed by your upbringing and shaped by life experience.

Bridge the gap by stepping into their world and validating their perspective.

Know that differing priorities don't necessarily have to be competing priorities. There can be space for your point, and there can also be room for theirs. Perspective shapes priorities. Priorities determine behavior. And for good measure, again I say: priorities determine behavior. Remember that. And also, "Shirley Goodness."

CHAPTER 4

ALL BEHAVIOR IS PURPOSEFUL

"And in all your getting, get understanding."
—Proverbs 4:7 (New King James Version)

Behavior is a form of communication. You may not always like what is being communicated, but there is meaning. It is a clue. So if we look at behavior as functional, considering the function of a particular behavior should inform how you decide to approach it.

In psychology, there is a theory by Edward Thorndike called the law of effect. It states that any behavior that is followed by a pleasant consequence is likely to be repeated, and any behavior followed by an unpleasant consequence is likely to be stopped.

As alluded to in the last chapter, behavior is a reflection of priorities. But as previously stated, the priorities of children and adults are often different. While this seems like a relatively practical notion to accept, there's also a biological component to it. The brain doesn't fully mature until our mid to late twenties. The frontal lobe, responsible for judgment, planning, assessing risks, and decision-making, is the last region to complete development.

As such, children are often incapable of the unrealistic expectations we place on them, and that can be reflected in their behavior. This brings me to my next point. . . .

Behavior is a manifestation of the abilities and tools in your child's toolbox. It is also important to understand that emotions often fuel behavior. That said, with my child, my goal is never to dictate *how* he should feel about something. However, my expectation is that he is able to exercise control in acknowledging those emotions and how he expresses them. I have to teach him that. But he can feel how he wants to feel.

As we get older, we learn more emotional granularity. According to psychologist Dr. Lisa Feldman Barrett, the emotionally wise person can create distinct experiences of disappointment, anger, spite, resentment, grouchiness, and aggravation, whereas for a less emotionally wise person, those are all synonyms for "I feel bad." It is our responsibility as parents to give our children the language to make sense of their emotions and appreciate the nuances therein.

This next concept is one that may be polarizing. But I believe that "bad behavior" isn't necessarily "bad." Kids aren't born bad. Sometimes they have bad surroundings, sometimes they are subject to ineffective parenting solutions, sometimes they have unmet needs, and sometimes it's a misalignment of priorities that, when interpreted, grates on your last nerve, or at the very least presents you with an inconvenient challenge. All of it falls under the umbrella of things that make *us* feel bad about what's happening. When children are exhibiting "bad behavior," sometimes it's helpful to ask: is there an environment that I can create or take my child to where their behavior would fit and be viewed more positively? If so, shift the environment. For instance, if your child tends to have sassy, quick comebacks when speaking to adults, perhaps signing them up for the school debate team would be a great way to channel that behavior.

When children are misbehaving, we may tend to blame it on a child's natural demeanor rather than think systematically about their familial, social, and community life, and how those factors may be influencing their actions. Behavior such as tantrums can indicate that your child is struggling to express strong emotions. This should signal to you that you need to help your child calm down before you can address the behavior. Envision a pendulum. A pendulum swings as far to the left as it does to the right. As a parent, you want to center your child. Give them some of your calm until they develop the ability to self-regulate. But recognize: this implies that you have to have some calm to offer them. As adults, we set the tone. When we lose our cool, most of what we say or do is completely lost on our children. All they learn when we're flailing is that they have the power to hurt us or ignite our rage, which unsettles them, and usually causes them to repeat their difficult behaviors until we find some control. According to psychotherapist and interpersonal biology expert Dr. Tina Payne Bryson, our chaos or calm are contagious, especially to those we spend the most time with.

Adults typically have more tools at their disposal, but let's face it: in reality, adults can have tantrum-like outbursts at any moment in time. In fact, you are probably able to imagine an example of this easily. Perhaps a situation with a particular coworker comes to mind. However, we do not typically refer to adults as having "tantrums." A mature adult should strive to have control over their emotions to help them maintain healthy relationships with the people they come into contact with on a daily basis. Ultimately, an adult tantrum happens when a grown-up cannot cope with negative emotions or calm themselves down. So for those adults, and for your children, don't get engaged in the tantrum. Do your best to remain calm. Trust me, I do not say this lightly. I have lived with a willful tiny human before. But you can't control their behavior; you can only control how you respond to it.

A tantruming child can make you feel like a failure and like you have lost control. What I have learned is that when children *are not* tantruming we only have the *illusion* of control. In actuality, I can't really control what my child does. The only person I can control is myself. However, I can tap into motivations to *influence* others. So this parenting pearl is not only applicable to toddlers but also to older children, and really, to people in general. When it comes to influence, there can be short-term gains and long-term gains. Because behaviors can become habits, I am about the long game. It is not my job to control; it is my job to guide. I aim to do so with patience and compassion. And let's really think about this: children don't enjoy tantrums. It is a form of release in response to being overwhelmed. The neuroscientist in me also bears in mind that child development is characterized by a continuum of executive function development which includes working memory, impulse control, emotional control, task initiation, planning and prioritizing, self-monitoring, organization, and flexible thinking. As such, there are some times when a child quite literally does not have the ability to behave differently because certain tools haven't yet developed. So, when I hear parents refer to their kids as "bad," it's the equivalent of me hearing fingernails on a chalkboard. In large part, I think "bad" kids are kids with *unmet needs*. Or in the words of psychologist Dr. Russell Barkley, "The kids who need the most love will ask for it in the most unloving ways." That does not excuse maladaptive behavior, but it does provide some context, grace, and insight if we understand that children seeking attention are requesting connection. Pam Leo of *Connection Parenting* says, "Either we spend time meeting children's emotional needs by filling their cup with love, or we spend time dealing with the behaviors caused from their unmet needs. Either way we spend the time."

Sometimes we lose sight of what it was like to be young. Children are entitled to bad days. And here's a news flash: *all* children will test limits. All of 'em! But believe in their goodness, and express gratitude for who they are. Every kid needs a champion. Why wouldn't that be you? What if you believe your child is brilliant and capable? Oh, how they would benefit from your view through that lens! Know that children *always* believe they deserve how we treat them. Always. Know also that we all, children and adults alike, act in a way that matches how we define ourselves. A child's first definition of themselves is formed by us.

As we continue to talk about behavior, let's consider the following concept: "There is no such thing as bad publicity." There is something fascinating about the parent-child dynamic such that, at any age, parental attention is a huge reward for the child. Sometimes, however, it doesn't matter what kind of attention you give your child. So a reaction to bad behavior is better than no attention at all. Even criticism or disciplining could feel like a reward to your child—and can actually lead to more bad behavior.

One possible solution is planned ignoring or tactical ignoring. (The caveat here is to ensure your child and their surroundings are safe for you to implement planned ignoring.) It is not about ignoring the child, but instead, the use of planned ignoring is about ignoring the behavior. Sometimes, no response is a response. To be clear, this is different from being dismissive. According to the *Oxford*

English Dictionary, to be dismissive is to show that something is unworthy of consideration. That, I would never suggest. However, I do recognize that parents are human, so there may be instances where you are intentionally or unintentionally dismissive. But your child is *always* worthy of consideration. Remember that. Planned ignoring is the equivalent of saying, "I'm not going to justify that with a response."

For example, if your child is laying in the middle of the living floor having a tantrum, don't look at them. Don't verbally engage them. Keep your face neutral. It may grate your nerves to see your child behave this way, but keep your resolve strong and do not give it attention. *As soon as* they calm down to the point where they can effectively receive communication from you, give it to them. Talk to them about how they are feeling. Give them your attention. *Show them* that desirable behavior gets your attention. This method can be particularly effective in young children. Furthermore, I recommend not punishing a child for having tantrums because it teaches them to stuff down their emotions instead of coping with their feelings in an appropriate way. When it comes to adolescents, sometimes your "ignoring" can actually be the reward, so use it wisely. But know that "no publicity" comes with a sting, so planned ignoring with older children (and even adults) can still be effective. Trust me.

If your child behaves in a particular way and gets your attention, your child is likely to behave that way again. But if you ignore the behavior, it is less likely to happen again. So attention for good behavior usually leads to more good behavior, and no attention for bad behavior usually leads to less bad behavior. Start ignoring when the maladaptive behavior begins, and stop ignoring *as soon as* the maladaptive behavior ceases. When you *consistently* give your child positive attention and praise for desired behavior, planned ignoring works better. Now here is where the village comes in. If someone else will provide the attention that you are taking away, then planned ignoring will not work as effectively. Whether it's your partner, a friend, or extended family, it is best to be on the same page. Understand that rewarding your child's maladaptive behavior some of the time will strengthen the behavior more than if the maladaptive behavior is rewarded every time it happens. This is because your child has to work harder for the response. I think the reason that parents sometimes end up reinforcing behaviors that they don't want their children to continue is simply because they are worn out! Parenting is hard! It is not for the faint of heart. And with this method in particular, consistency is key. All that said, there is a caveat—please do not ignore dangerous or destructive behavior! Safety first.

- While planned ignoring uses reinforcement and other strategies to help children learn and acquire new adaptive behaviors, I do want to provide an alternative. Though I have employed some planned ignoring in my own parenting at times, admittedly, I have mixed feelings about it. Child psychologist and author, Dr. Mona Delhooke, does as well. She notes that there is often great frustration in trying to make oneself understood. Not uncommonly, tantrums and other maladaptive behaviors are a reflection of that. The concern with planned ignoring is that it doesn't build social and emotional development when we ignore a child's attempts to communicate. Instead, it can fuel a child's frustration, anger, and resentment. We must ask ourselves, if behaviors are a form of communication, what message are we giving by ignoring them? According to Dr. Delhooke, there are some hidden costs of this commonly used tool:

- Ignoring sends the wrong emotional message to the child. In short, the adult is saying, "I'm not interested in what you're trying to convey, and I'll pay attention only when you comply with my demands."

- Ignoring presupposes that a child's observable behaviors accurately reveal his or her intentions. In fact, many children, depending upon their age and stage of development, lack the ability to coordinate movement and/or language to convey their inner thoughts.

- Ignoring oversimplifies the child's behaviors without trying to discern underlying thoughts and feelings.

Furthermore, when I think about the word *responsibility*, I think about the ability to be responsive. So, I want to be available to my child when they're most upset. I want them to know that our relationship is not conditional. I want them to know that they are not only acceptable to me when they please me. I want my actions to translate into stability and reliability. Dr. Delhooke implores us to have compassion for our child and ourselves, and assume the child wants to please us but can't in the moment. She recommends that we reframe the behavior and promote relational safety. For younger and older children alike, we can ask ourselves, "How can I help make it easier for this child to communicate with me?" This kind of relationship-based approach considers the child's emotions and relationships as the foundation for interaction.

I've said it before and I'll say it again, parenting is hard! It's not a one-size-fits-all type of deal. Nor is it a one-method-fits-all-scenarios type of deal. I think what's most important is to trust your instinct as a parent. If a certain technique doesn't feel right for your child, figure out a new one. Another consideration to be mindful of is this: Letting our behavior be consistent with our beliefs and feelings. It is a way for parents to model what they want their kids to do. So, toss out the antiquated notion of, "Do as I say, not as I do." Telling your kids is one thing; *showing* them is another. Choose what you show.

CHAPTER 5

BASIC NEEDS

"A deep sense of love and belonging are irreducible needs of all men, women, and children. In the absence of love and belonging, there is always suffering. We are biologically, cognitively, physically, and spiritually wired to love, to be loved, and to belong."

—Brené Brown

There are many theories about healthy development. One of these developmental models is Maslow's Hierarchy of Needs. It is a psychological theory of motivation originally developed in 1943 by the psychologist Abraham Maslow that argues that humans have different levels of needs. Needs indicate priorities. And as discussed in Chapter 3, priorities determine behavior. But let's get back to Maslow. The five stages are typically displayed as a pyramid. Each intermediary level builds upon the level below it. There are basic needs at the bottom of the pyramid, and more high-level, intangible needs at the top. Maslow regarded the needs toward the bottom of the pyramid as "deficiency needs" because they arise due to inadequacies or deprivation. According to his theory, if you fail to meet your deficiency needs, you will experience unpleasant results. Needs toward the top of the hierarchy, e.g., self-actualization, represent "growth needs." Such needs do not stem from a lack of something, but instead reflect the need to grow as a person. A person can only move on to addressing the higher-level needs when their basic needs are adequately fulfilled. Unmet growth needs are not harmful if left unfulfilled.

At the base of the pyramid are basic *biological and physiological needs* such as food, water, shelter, clothing, warmth, and sleep. These needs are at the core of what is needed to function as a human being. They are essential to our survival. These needs must first be met before children can advance to any other level. For example, if children are hungry or tired, they have a far more difficult time concentrating on more complex situations. Anyone that has experience with infants and toddlers inherently knows this. It is why a feeling of intense panic envelopes you if you forget the diaper bag at home, with their bottle, even if the trip to the grocery store with your little one is intended to be quick. As my mother always says, "It's better to have it and not need it than to need it and not have it." So, if you don't have that bottle when that baby's lips are smacking, then you might as well consider the trip to the store an epic fail because "good" behavior henceforth is not guaranteed. This is why it is wise to attend to these basic requirements first, before encouraging children to play, listen to a story, complete work, or engage in other activities. The example provided with a baby is relatable, but this holds true for children old enough to fend for themselves, and for adults as well. For instance, food insecurity and inadequate shelter are ugly realities here in the United States and in many parts of the world. So know that these unmet basic needs may exist even if the presentation isn't what you would expect. Respond accordingly.

Safety needs comprise the second stage and deal with the need for stability, security, protection, and freedom from fear. To thrive and live healthy lives, humans need a sense of safety. This includes physical safety as well as emotional and psychological safety. Safety isn't just the absence of a threat, but the presence of connection. In fact, the brain of a child who feels emotionally or physically threatened produces chemicals that actually inhibit learning. Threat or stress put the brain in survival mode at the expense of higher-order thinking skills. Lasting threats or stress reduce the brain's capacity for understanding, meaning, memory, and analytical thinking. A development tool called the Mandt System asserts that safety and security can be summarized as "consistency and predictability." Therefore, it is vital that we support our children by ensuring that the conditions necessary for learning are in place. Humans, and especially kids, *thrive* in routine and an environment in which they are comfortable. Once a child's initial needs are met, they may be more aware of their additional needs in this stage.

The next stage, *love and belongingness*, deals with affection, love, friendship, connectedness, and inclusivity. We all have an innate need to give and receive love and to give and receive care. Therefore, a life without healthy relationships is not a healthy life. Healthy relationships can be defined as relationships that are emotionally, physically, psychologically, or spiritually sound. Here, children will be able to make friends or connect with their loved ones. Everyone wants to feel important to somebody sometimes, and children have an essential need to belong in an attachment relationship where they feel safe and secure and are free from having to work. This means that they don't have to work in order for the relationship to work. They don't have to be good or smart or pretty or compliant—they should just be. They need rest from having to work to be accepted. A caring, affirming adult can make all the difference. What is at the heart of a sense of belonging is whether or not you're being fed by the space you're in. You cannot thrive in a famine.

Higher up in the pyramid is the fourth stage, *esteem*, which revolves around children's need to gain independence, self-respect, or achievements. We tend to think of achievement as something that adults seek out but not kids. This is not true. Children benefit from being praised for their work or being able to accomplish something on their own. Sometimes, well-intentioned parents need to be reminded not to rob their children of experiences that allow them to do something on their own. This also includes allowing them to make mistakes (excluding circumstances involving danger or high likelihood of disfigurement). Sometimes, as a parent, it can be painful to watch them make mistakes. But I assure you that this experiential learning is so critical. Kids need to achieve just as much as adults do. Their achievements are just different and developmentally appropriate. For example, an achievement for a five-year-old may be coloring a picture "within the lines," which often provides a feeling best characterized by the phrase, "I did it!"

Finally, there is the stage of *self-actualization*. This deals with the realization of personal potential or self-fulfillment. This can also be thought of as a child's ability to rise, to act creatively, to dream, to act without fear, and to find purpose. This develops over time and deals with a sense of contentment with oneself and one's situation. Naturally, this is particularly challenging for young children to comprehend; however, if we go back to one of the goals listed in Chapter 1 regarding preparation for adulthood, at some point parents need to help their children look inward to recognize the awesomeness that we've known they possess all along.

In summary, once the basic human needs are met, then safety and security needs can be met, then relationship needs can be met; once relationship needs are met, achievement needs can be met, and finally, once all other needs are met, the need for self-actualization can be met. Now take a step back. Can you think of a scenario where a need at any one of these tiers hasn't been met? If you can't—how do I put this nicely? You're delusional. If you found that offensive, I assure you it would be less so if you weren't, for instance, hangry. Conditions ranging from illness and starvation, up through loneliness and self-doubt, are the byproducts of unmet deficiency needs. So presuming that you can imagine children experiencing deficiencies with this lens, I'm sure you can understand why I am adamant about considering the whole child when I approach my patients. I encourage you to do the same in encounters with your children. Further, I think you will find that mindfulness around these principles can be quite useful across the entire lifespan and can inform many of your other relationships.

CHAPTER 6

CHALLENGES

"Avoiding conflict is a way of avoiding connection."
—Unknown

You see the word "challenges" and likely have a visceral response. So let me start off by saying that challenges are opportunities. Challenges test our faith and help us grow. Challenges are evidence that an opportunity exists to do something differently OR to adjust your way of being. Don't get me wrong, "different" can be daunting. I do not always view challenges with enthusiasm, especially not initially. Eventually though, I can usually get to a place where I can see the silver lining. Additionally, I've realized that challenges in the parent-child dynamic can often be grouped into one of seven categories:

1. Tolerating "No" and Handling Disappointment

2. Delayed Gratification

3. Misalignment of Expectations

4. Responsibility

5. Accountability

6. Transitions

7. Failures and Losses

Keep these themes in mind. Oftentimes, being able to frame your experiences in a more manageable way can make the challenge, whatever it may be, seem possible and surmountable. Furthermore, when you recognize the opportunity that your challenge presents, you find your reward. There are lessons in the valleys and in the rain.

In addition to the seven categories, sometimes it can also be helpful to view challenges in terms of unmet needs. What is the unmet need that has to be alleviated for the desired outcome? Or perhaps you can ask yourself: is negativity going to linger by responding or reacting in a certain way? Your role is to discern. Act with discernment. When you have a different response during a moment of challenge, you create a foundation upon which to build different resources so that future moments of challenge can be different. Additionally, I have found it helpful to focus on my child's understanding when it comes to facing challenges. One of the things I have learned from my child is to not rush his understanding. What I mean by that is, when I talk to him in a pressured and frustrated kind of way, it is the surest way for me to not get through to him. Instead, if I shift my focus from what I want to what he needs in that moment, it's better for the both of us. But don't get me wrong—unpolished, impassioned, urgent communication certainly has its place. Outside of that, if I see that he's not understanding something, instead of getting frustrated or trying to rush him through, I offer him patience and tenderness. That's where many opportunities for growth live for him. I imagine that this is true for other children as well.

CHAPTER 7

BE INTENTIONAL

"All things are a manifestation of thought.
Speak life into children."

—Unknown

Try as we might, no childhood will be completely devoid of trauma. Trauma is a wound you sustain that shows up later on in life. According to Dr. Gabor Mate, physician and expert on childhood development and trauma, you can wound a child in two ways—you can do bad things to them, or you can deprive them of their needs—the latter being the good things that didn't happen to them that should've. What I also know is that whatever a kid sees frequently becomes their normal. This is why toxicity can be tolerated and repeated in subsequent relationships. And it is for all of these reasons and more that I firmly believe that intentionality is key.

Children "build" a brain that is best suited to the environment they experience. Our brains prepare us to expect certain experiences by forming the pathways needed to respond to those experiences.

We create pathways in the brain by behaving in certain ways. The amazing thing about the brain is that it's made to rewire itself all the time. This is a phenomenon called neuroplasticity. Scientists used to think that after childhood, our brains stop changing, but we now know that our brain changes depending upon how we use it. According to neuroscientist Dr. Pat Levitt, research shows that early life experiences influence social skills, emotional skills, and learning skills. Healthy brain architecture provides the resilience to deal with adversity experienced during the first years of life, and the aforementioned skills come together to help children succeed in the real world. So if there were just one thing I could impress upon all of the parents that I come across, it's that parents shape what their children will be willing to do for attention, affection, approval, and consideration. Let that simmer.

Parents, good or bad, you are influential. There is an inherent trust in the parent-child relationship that even when it gets broken, there is always space for grace and possibility that is unlike any other human relationship. While intent and impact are two different things, at least intent takes into consideration the impact you *may* have. You don't have to be perfect. Nor does everything have to be planned. But know that consideration goes a long way. And even if children can't quite articulate consideration, they can perceive it. They can discern when consideration for them exists, and when it is lacking. The extent to which your impact has long-lasting influence we will never know, but I assure you, good or bad, you *are* influential. So be intentional. Our children are at the mercy of our bad habits, our emotions, our toxicity.

I'm not here to preach perfect parenting. I'm here to uphold the humanness of the people fulfilling that role. That's where intention comes in. There is power in intention. The intention informs the cause. Before you have an action, there is a reason for you taking that action, and the reason for you taking that action will show up in your life on the other end. Our children deserve more than haphazard offerings of us. When there is clarity of intention, our children benefit.

Another point that I'd like to touch on is the old saying, "You are a product of your environment." I do believe there is merit to that. Frequently, this adage spills over into a debate on nature versus nurture. Well, the environment is the nature piece. I also believe the following: "You are a product of your expectations." That's the nurture piece. It's why I like to speak life into every child I meet, and it's another reason why I encourage parents to be intentional. Sometimes, we base our worth on how other people respond to us, and children are particularly susceptible to this. In the words of Wes Moore, "The expectations that we all have of ourselves don't come from nowhere. They come from the expectations that other people have of us. And we internalize them and make them our own." You'd be surprised how many kids don't have a good grasp on what their parents expect of them out of life. So first of all, have some expectations. The rest of the world will be expecting something of your child—I assure you. Whether the expectations are "low" or "high" is all relative. But as a parent, your expectations are some of the ones that will matter most to your child. So remember, your child is a product, not only of their environment, but also of their expectations.

CHAPTER 8

MAKE WAY FOR DUCKLINGS

"Time is a decision."
—Dr. Kimberly Reynolds

One day I was doing some chores with the TV on in the background, so I was only halfway paying attention to the television. But in this particular show, there was a little boy who had experienced some traumatic circumstances and was subsequently placed in emergency custody. Throughout the show, he exhibited some rude and rebellious behavior, but there was an adult male figure with whom he developed a bond while he was in emergency custody. Toward the end of the episode, a woman comes to take him to the foster family that had been located for him. The kid is saddened and distraught. He starts apologizing profusely for his bad behavior and promises to be good if he can stay with the guy that he has taken a liking to. You can see the turmoil pulling on this guy's heartstrings. He tries to explain to the boy why he has to go with the lady to meet his new foster family. It's still difficult for him to understand, but the boy reluctantly accepts his fate. He starts to walk toward the woman, but stops, turns back, and gives the guy the book in his hand, *Make Way for Ducklings*. It's obvious that the guy is deeply moved by this gesture, but he tries to give the boy back his book because he knows how much he enjoys it. The boy insists that the guy keep it, so he does, and they part ways.

This scene really caught my attention. It made me pause and reflect on the heart and concept of giving what you can. Sometimes, little kids give us things that mean a lot to them. Though small, it's precious, and we appreciate it because we recognize that it's what they have to give. Similarly, children are very attuned to us and whether or not we give what we can. I think all parents experience guilt in some way, shape, or form when it comes to the time, energy, and effort that we must devote to our employment or other things not directly related to our children. We miss them when we're gone. They miss us. I get it. But this isn't to shame people that work, especially people that work a lot. However, what I can tell you is that kids pay attention to what you do with them and how you engage with them at those times when you *can* be around. What does that look like? Are you present? In the words of Daniel Tiger, my advice is to "enjoy the 'wow' that's happening now."

In conversations with adult children, one of the things that stands out is the capacity that they had as children to understand that Mommy or Daddy had to work. *But* they cherished those times when mom or dad showed up. They knew you were tired. They recognized you were busy. But ultimately, you made a choice. You chose them. And *that* is what matters. What I'm speaking to is the issue of giving what you can. An example of the way that this has played out with me is when I was dead tired after a night shift and I didn't have the energy to play with my son. Did I feel terrible about that? Yes. But what I could do was cuddle with him in my bed, let him enjoy PBS Kids on the iPad, and pause his show periodically to ask questions, talk to him, and show him that I'm sharing interest in what he's interested in. So it wasn't ideal. I know that he would have preferred for us to be actively playing on the floor or going to the park, but it's what I could do. It's what I was able to give in that moment.

For families where both parents perhaps don't live in the same household, time and time again, a grievance that children develop centers around the perceived choice that you had when you didn't show up. Sporadically making contact when it's convenient for you, but not when your child needs you, leaves a trauma wound on the child that can affect them their entire life. So it may not be perfect, but give what you can, when you can give it. Make connection a habit. For all parents and parent-proxies, I say to you, you don't have to be a perfect parent to be a good parent. But you do have to be present. How do you show up for your children?

With children of any age really, love is spelled t-i-m-e. So even for the parents holding down more than one job, I've seen enough kids to know that they can be adaptable and they can come to understand that you have to be gone. But what sticks out most is how you spend your time when you can be around. Believe it or not, at an early age, kids understand the power of choice.

PART I P3Q's

- What was a turning point in your childhood when you decided you wanted to set yourself apart from something a parental figure had done?

- What was a turning point in your childhood when you decided you wanted to emulate something a parental figure had done?

- Who in your childhood made you feel significant, and how did you know you were significant to them?

- What do you admire about your child? Is there something you can name that divorces them from their accomplishments? Do they know how you feel?

- Do you know what your kids care about?

- What would you say is the hallmark of your parenting style? Does your execution match your intent?

- What do you hope your kids see when it comes to healthy relationships? Is this represented by you or others in the village?

- What dynamics have you modeled for your kids that you think you've done really well?

- What behaviors have you modeled for your kids that you hope they don't replicate?

PART II:
THE SPECIFICS

Note: I embrace the LGBTQ community, and I recognize that gender is not binary. The general way that we discuss gender is a construct. Admittedly though, the trans, gender nonconforming, and gender non-binary experience are within my awareness yet outside of my expertise. I acknowledge my limitations, and it is not my intention to exclude children or parents who identify in this way. For the purposes of this text, I will be discussing gender from a masculine and feminine perspective in the next two chapters. To that end, I want to highlight that, to some degree, we are all influenced by concepts of masculinity and femininity. So regardless of your gender identity, you may be able to relate to some of the experiences described here.

CHAPTER 9

FROGS AND SNAILS AND PUPPY DOG TAILS

"We are dangerous when we are not conscious of our responsibility for how we behave, think, and feel."
—Marshall B. Rosenberg

It is not uncommon for many children with a masculine identity to grow up in an emotionally unsafe environment. To survive the early years, boys are often conditioned to shut down their ability to feel their emotions within their physical bodies. Their consciousness as it relates to how they feel is suppressed, along with their empathy for others. For many, the remaining "acceptable" emotions that boys are allowed to feel are anger and happiness. And with that mandate, boys can be happy sometimes, but if they are not, then society tells us that boys are supposed to be tough and aggressive. Among other "acceptable" forms of masculinity are fearlessness, not asking for help, having power over others, being hypersexual, and using violence to get respect. Basically, "men" are always in control, always right, always ready to fight, and always ready to f*%k. (Excuse my crassness; sorry Mom!) This represents a collective socialization of males that we all have been taught on some level. As such, men and boys are left living within the rigid confines of masculinity that do not honor the fullness of their humanity. So what happens when they experience more nuanced emotions? The mere interrogation of this notion is an affront to the prevailing definitions of masculinity.

Ted Bunch is the co-founder and chief development officer of A Call to Men, an organization that aims to promote healthy and respectful manhood. They have coined the term the "Man Box," which represents the collective socialization of men. According to psychologist and author of *How to Raise A Boy*, Dr. Michael Reichert, the attitudes embodied in the Man Box are seriously harming boys and men. Furthermore, they also impact the level of respect and safety imparted to women, girls, and those at the margins of society. Dr. Reichert goes on to say that those guys in the Man Box are "the most unhappy, the most anxious, the most vulnerable to both being bullies and being bullied, the most often perpetrators of sexual assault and sexual harassment, and the most often prone to suicidal thinking." That for me is enough to want to do something differently. But the research is also quite clear. At the outset of life, boys and girls experience the same emotions just as vividly, just as profoundly. So it is not the experience of emotions that's different between males and females—it's the expression of emotion. The expression of emotion follows what we call "feeling rules." Those feeling rules are culture. We tell girls, "Don't be angry. Be a lady." We tell boys, "Don't be scared. Don't be vulnerable. Don't cry. Don't be weak. Be strong. Be stoic. Keep it inside." That is so profoundly damaging to how we actually keep our minds present. And in the words of world-renowned therapist Marisa Peer, "Males express themselves the least and kill themselves the most." It's clear, the Man Box has a hefty ransom.

One of the antidotes for toxic masculinity is to be in relationship with others who respect your sensitivity. For this to happen, you must first respect it in yourself and not uphold gendered ideas of emotional repression. Dr. Reichert believes that adults are responsible for changing the narrative and creating a healthier environment for boys to thrive. I tend to agree. He says, "We are the ones that created boyhood, not our boys. We're the ones that are managing boyhood. Males as well as females. If we want to change the outcomes that boyhood produces, we can't look to the boys. We actually have to look to us and the message that we give them."

Being a member of society, I have perpetuated some of these ideals. Also, moving through society as a female, I have been on the receiving end of the way that this harm manifests itself. So, one of the things that I am adamant about is allowing my son to express a full range of emotions. It requires a lot of intentionality because I too have been fed the false narrative of how males should behave. However, early in my son's existence, I realized that empowering him to acknowledge his emotions, and then giving him the language to understand and speak about his emotions, is one of the most important acts of love I can muster. So despite what the world says, at the very least, in our home, he knows that his wholeness is honored.

CHAPTER 10

SUGAR AND SPICE AND EVERYTHING NICE

"To be yourself in a world that is constantly trying to make you something else is the greatest accomplishment."
—Ralph Waldo Emerson

I am the mother to a son, no daughters, at least not yet. However, I do have my thoughts about what is most important when it comes to raising girls. After all, I used to be a girl, and I have the lived experience of what a girl grows to become. As such, one of the most beneficial things I try to do for my nieces is to praise them for attributes not related to appearance. Do I think that they are cute? Absolutely. Do they have pretty dresses and pretty bows? Sure. But I already know that the world will teach them that these external delights are where much of their worth comes from. I want them to know that they are more than a beautiful face or an attractive body (whatever that means for the prevailing trends).

As girls advance in their womanhood, I am sure they will at some point feel vulnerable in the face of gender expectations. I want them to know who they are, irrespective of the male gaze and regardless of male approval. The desire to be pretty and to be liked may reign supreme for a season. I get it. But as long as they know that their physicality is not the sum of their validation, then I'm good with that. Because we also live in a society that equates beauty with youth, I would want them to know that their worth does not wane after they surpass a particular age. Fading beauty is not fading worth. True beauty is in their substance of being. So if there was only one piece of advice, just one piece, that I could give a young lady I care about, I would say this: You better know who you are, baby girl, because a lot of people are willing to let you borrow their ideas of you at your expense until you figure it out.

CHAPTER 11

ON BODILY AUTONOMY
AND ABUSE

"You don't have the language to begin to explain what's happening to you. That's why you feel you're not going to be believed. And if the abuser, the molester, is any good, they will make you feel that you are complicit, that you were part of it. That's what keeps you from telling."

—Oprah Winfrey

Check this out. I ask my son if I can hug him or kiss him. Yes. The fruit of my womb. Yes. The child that I carried for thirty-nine weeks and endured nearly twenty-four hours of labor for. I ask him if I can hug him or kiss him. If he says "No," I don't do it. It doesn't matter what I thought he meant. It doesn't matter what I wanted to hear. It doesn't matter how irresistibly cute his cheeks are, or how snuggly I find him to be. If he says "No," I stop. The pediatrician in me is adamant about this. I do this because I want to set an example for dismantling rape culture. I also respect his "No" because I want him to know that his voice matters. If this is the expectation he has in our home, it is my hope that it helps him find his voice in the world. It is my hope that it also translates into the way that he treats others. "No's" should be respected—regardless of age, size, or relationship.

The larger concept operating here is one of bodily autonomy. Body autonomy is the right for a person to govern what happens to their body without external influence or coercion. This is an important concept for all children to be taught and to understand. Why? Because as a pediatrician, the ugly part of my job is dealing with child abuse, of which there are various types. While I recognize that the idea of abuse happening to our children is very difficult to accept, here's what I know: A child who knows that they are in control of their body is less likely to fall victim to sexual abuse, sexual assault, and later, to intimate partner violence. They are also more likely to disclose any abusive events that should happen to them. Here, it is important to also recognize one of the myriad reasons why a child might not disclose abuse. It is a sentiment that I have heard echoed from the mouths of children as well as from adults who later disclose their abuse. When a child has been in an abusive situation, they often don't want to tell their parents because they don't want their parents to think that they have let them down in any way, or they fear not being believed, or they don't want to feel responsible for igniting extreme levels of upset in their parents nor feel responsible for any subsequent retaliation toward the perpetrator. We must reassure our kids that our feelings do not require this type of protection, nor do our feelings trump their lived experience.

As adults, we are positioned to help prevent abuse from happening to our kids, and to empower them to disclose it if it does. It is our responsibility to cultivate a sense of confidence and personal agency. Yet all too often, adults force children into situations in which their bodies are treated as the property of others. For example, it does not matter if it has been a year since your child has seen a certain family member. If it does not happen organically, they should not be forced to hug them. There are alternate ways to show respect and affection. Or instead, for example, if a pre-verbal child winces or tries to escape your affection, honor what they are showing you. And if a child declines your affection, do not make them responsible for your feelings. Do not dramatically orchestrate your disappointment as though you are owed their affection on your terms. Do not coerce them. Do not guilt them. The reason that I am adamant about this philosophy is because it is a way to protect them from abuse. It's not something that any of us like to think about, but it happens. And I assure you, it happens way more often than you think. One out of every three girls and one out of every twenty boys will experience unwanted sexual contact by their eighteenth birthday. These are just the reported incidences. *And,* the people that will perpetrate this violence, in most cases unfortunately, are people that that child knows and trusts.

All that said, I know that one of the most important things I can teach my son is that he has agency over his own body. I believe that all kids should be affirmed in this way, to the extent that I *always* do my best to impart this to every child that is a patient of mine. All children have the need and the right to be protected from every form of violence, victimization, and neglect. It doesn't matter if someone is older, bigger, or stronger than you. It doesn't matter if they are usually nice to you. You should be able to have a say in what happens to your body.

CHAPTER 12

HIGHWATERS AND SNUG SHOES

"Maturity is a high price to pay for growing up."
—Tom Stoppard

I had always heard about how teenagers will eat you out of house and home, but I wasn't ready for my five-year-old to do it! This child ate an entire cauliflower pizza! While I was happy about the sneaky vegetable intake, I felt like I had inadequately stocked my freezer. It's tough to keep up! Even though I see him every day, I marvel at how much he has grown, and at how fast it's all happening. I find myself also marveling at the frequency with which wardrobe changes are necessary—and not to keep up with the latest fad, but simply to have items that fit properly. Just the other day, I went into my child's drawer to grab some pants for him to put on. He puts them on, and they look a little small, so I grab another pair. He puts those on, and those are small. I grab a third pair, and you've guessed it—those pants are looking small too! They are a little tight, and his ankles are showing. I exclaim to myself, "All of my baby's pants are highwaters!" Now for those of you not familiar with the term, "highwaters" is a Maryland colloquialism that describes unintentionally short pants that can theoretically be worn in a flood without getting wet. Thankfully, the weather was appropriate for my son to wear shorts instead.

Fast-forward to another day. My son just returned from a neighborhood walk with dad. The guys return home, and hubby helps the kiddo take off his shoes. Hubby then turns to me and says, "His toes are crunched up." A smile unfolds across my face, and my brow quizzically furrows, to which he says, "When is the last time you checked how his feet fit in these shoes?" I honestly couldn't recall how long it had been. His growth caught both hubby and me by surprise. It seemed like we had just purchased those shoes only a short while ago, and now it was time to size up again. Admittedly, I chuckled at my child's "wardrobe malfunction." Meanwhile, in his youthful innocence my child is still beaming because he got to go outside and is now ready to run upstairs and play with his toys, not caring at all about his clothes or shoes. I, on the other hand, began to reflect on the saying, "The days are long, but the years are short." I came to the realization that at different stages of life, I grieve for different things. I've become more aware of the marked passage of time. I am proud of, amused by, and excited about the kid that my son is growing to be, but I grieve the infant and toddler days, just a little. In that moment, I recognized the need to pause and process how quickly time is flying by. You should, too.

CHAPTER 13

ON SEX

"Curiosity in children is but an appetite for knowledge."
—John Locke

We have to talk about this. It is a topic that tends to cause parents and parent-proxies great angst, "How do I talk about it?" "When do I talk about it?" And so on. You can easily become engulfed in a spiraling list of quandaries about how to broach this topic. I understand. The conversation surrounding sex encompasses many things. It's body parts; it's body changes—hair, smells, and secretions; it's feelings, urges, and desires; it's social norms; it's sexual choices and consequences. As a pediatrician, it is quite common for me to help initiate these conversations or lend support for the discussion to continue. I recognize that sex can be tied to religious ideals, and it can also be politicized. *That* aspect of the conversation I always leave to the parents and parent-proxies. I don't care about that. But there are concepts that I want ALL parents to know and consider when it comes to talking about sex, so keep reading.

First and foremost, it is not a one-off conversation. It needs to be an ongoing discussion that gets revisited. And by discussion, that means that the adult shouldn't just be talking *at* the child. There needs to be space for the child to ask questions. The conversation should also be age-appropriate.

Second, if you start the conversation at puberty, you are starting much too late. The conversation should actually start around kindergarten age by talking about body parts. Calling it "down there" or "privates" is not sufficient. To be clear, I also am not in favor of teaching kids to call their body parts by "cute" names. While some of those names are unmistakably indicative of what we're talking about, others are more vague. I believe in calling it what it is. We're talking about vulva, vagina, penis, testicles, and buttocks. Call it what it is. We must use proper names because it eliminates confusion. We don't want kids to be confused about their bodies. Occasionally I hear parents or parent-proxies express concern about the child's ability to properly say the appropriate names of genitalia. Trust that the wonderful capabilities your kindergartener has to acquire other languages is the same capacity they have to learn the appropriate names. Don't set them up for confusion. But also, don't set yourself up for confusion. In Chapter 11, we discussed preventing abuse by teaching bodily autonomy. Using the appropriate terms for genitalia is another way to prevent abuse. If a child is talking about their vagina or someone else's, I as an adult want to know about it. If a child is talking about their penis or someone else's, I as an adult want to know about it. If I were to overhear a child say "purse" or "jewels" I would have no way of knowing whether or not they're talking about where I store my money when I'm out shopping or what I wear on my neck and wrist when I want to look fancy. So if someone is grooming them with age-inappropriate conversation, or if someone is touching them inappropriately, I don't want there to be any delay or ambiguity when it comes to me being clued in on what is happening. Normalizing the proper anatomical terms protects from predators and misinformation. Another point that I'd like to make here is this: Please refrain from using the terms "good touch" and "bad touch." Instead, say "appropriate touch" and "inappropriate touch." Because the truth of the matter is that "bad" (as in inappropriate) touches can sometimes feel good. So again, let's eliminate the confusion and mitigate some of the shame that violated children often feel.

Third, it is helpful for parents and parent-proxies to accept the fact that, at some point, their kids will have sex, whether for reproductive reasons or social reasons. The percentage of lifelong virgins is miniscule. So accepting the fact that sex will happen, my requirements for sex are SEC. Sex should be safe. Sex should be enjoyable. Sex should be consensual. That's it. And here's the thing about consent. Consent is as easy as FRIES. Consent is freely given. Consent is reversible. Consent is informed. Consent is enthusiastic. Consent is specific. FRIES.

CHAPTER 14

ON FINANCIAL FOUNDATIONS

*"Consider this—money will have a greater influence
on your life than almost any other commodity you
can think of."*

—Bob Proctor

Let me start off by acknowledging that this can be an emotional topic. Be that as it may, we mustn't shy away from it. Let me also state that this chapter is not about to delve into the specifics of stocks and bonds. You would be better served seeking such knowledge from an expert in that arena, of which I am not. However, what we will discuss briefly is the mindset necessary for financial foundations to flourish.

I want parents to know that they are *crucial* in influencing their child's relationship with money. Financial prosperity is less about how you manage your funds, and more about how you manage your beliefs. Affording the life you want for yourself and your children comes down to what values you choose to pass down. This is not to negate the myriad of other factors that influence personal finance, but more so to emphasize the importance of one's financial beliefs. Beliefs influence priorities. As you know from Chapter 3, priorities determine behavior. Simply put, your behaviors surrounding money, the decisions you make regarding money, and how you choose to engage with money are reflections of what you think about money and what you learned about money. What is considered "rich" is relative. I felt I had a rich upbringing because my parents made very clear exactly what we valued and what we prioritized as a family. Raising a family that will feel rich no matter how much you can afford will depend upon how you choose to prioritize your needs and wants, which is related to your beliefs, which then influence how you manage your money.

Whatever financial path you choose to take as a parent, do not keep it to yourself! Involve your kids. This is how financial literacy is fostered. Communicate to them the *deliberate* choices you are making and why. Because at some point in time, your kids will become curious about money. As soon as they begin to observe how others are spending and saving, they will have questions for you. I recommend asking them why they are curious, because it will provide you with necessary context for the conversation. Your child's curiosity is a great catalyst for teaching them about money. So leverage these moments to help your kids manage their expectations, and when they're older, to plan appropriately.

The truth is that the standard education system does not teach simple money management tactics to children growing up. We have to fill in the gap. If you are someone who isn't financially savvy, rest assured that many people are not, and know that there is no shame in being willing to learn! Just take your kids on your journey to financial confidence. Please also keep in mind these words of Bob Proctor, author of *You Were Born Rich* and several other books: "People don't feel comfortable about money because they have it; they have it because they feel comfortable about it." Helping your kids feel comfortable about it is one of the best things that you can do.

CHAPTER 15

ON NOURISHMENT

"Hunger knows no friend but its feeder."
—Aristophanes

Think about one of your favorite foods. You are likely smiling as your imagination dances with this memory. One of the reasons that it's a favorite is obviously because it tastes delicious. Yet I wouldn't be surprised if another reason that it's your favorite is because of the person(s) and experiences attached to your memory of this food. For me, one of my favorite foods is bread pudding. Not only is it delicious and not overly sweet, but it makes me think of my grandmother because she used to make it for me. So for me, bread pudding is satiety, nostalgia, and comfort.

In addition to my dessert preferences, another little-known fact about me is that once upon a time, prior to medical school, I used to work as a certified personal trainer. I absolutely loved it! For one, I was in the best physical shape of my life. Secondly, I loved working with motivated people on their fitness goals. Creating exercise routines, advising on meal plans, providing accountability, and seeing the success of my clients was quite fulfilling. Through that line of work, through my later role as a pediatrician, and through a multitude of other conversations and observations, I know that a huge part of food choice is familial context. This means that parents and parent-proxies have tremendous power to form children's tastes. One of the main things we know about taste is that liking is a consequence of familiarity. So the more we expose children to nutritionally dense options, the greater the chance that they will learn to like healthy foods.

Another important consideration is the eating behaviors that we inherit. We learn to feed through our parents who probably rewarded us with food. Because the food and the love are so bound up, it is sometimes hard to see where the sugar ends and the love begins. Other motivational factors driving food preferences include culture, memory, and early feeding patterns. Parents' food preferences and eating behaviors provide an opportunity to model good eating habits. The implications are far-reaching. Children model themselves on their parents' eating behaviors, lifestyles, eating-related attitudes, and dissatisfaction regarding body image. Childhood eating behaviors are attracting increasing interest in nutrition research because poor diet quality at a young age and deviations from optimal weight have been associated with an increased risk of developing chronic diseases such as diabetes, obesity, and cardiovascular disease later in life. So as you can see, giving our kids fond memories associated with nutritious food is the gift that keeps on giving. Sharing nutritious food with your family then becomes an everyday act of love.

CHAPTER 16

GRACE TO GROW

*"You will teach them to fly,
but they will not fly your flight.
You will teach them to dream,
but they will not dream your dream.
You will teach them to live,
but they will not live your life.
Nevertheless,
in every flight, in every life, in every dream,
the print of the way you taught them will remain."*

—Commonly attributed to Mother Teresa

Some of the life experiences I cherish most are the times when I got to study abroad. Interestingly enough, the first time I ever went on an airplane I was sixteen years old. It just so happens that my first plane ride was also my first transatlantic trip. I was on my way to Italy! How cool is that! I was in my high school's gospel choir, and our phenomenal choir director, Ruth Jones, arranged a tour for us to sing across Italy, France, and Spain. Naturally, I wanted to go. Naturally, cost aside, my parents had some concerns. My maternal grandmother in particular had even *more* concerns, and my mom certainly got an earful about it. I can't say that I was privy to all of the discussions that were had, but I do know that my mom was a fierce advocate for me. I also know the source of her advocacy. My mom, a worldly and well-traveled woman, never got to travel much prior to adulthood. And one of her biggest regrets is not going away to college. My grandmother wanted her to stay close to home, so she did. She stayed at home, attended a local university, and obtained her associate degree.

Though my mom and my grandma always had a very close relationship, I know that at times my mom felt restricted because my grandmother held on to her so tightly. Upon reflection, what I realized is that part of what my mom longed for was the grace to grow. But I believe that with the understanding she had of the world at the time, my grandmother, who had never traveled beyond the East Coast of the United States, acted in the best way she knew how. Later, through her career, my mom developed quite the impressive passport. So when the opportunity came around for me to travel abroad, the lens my mom had was very different from my grandmother's.

Of course, there are dangers at home, as well as abroad, but my mom knew that there was a richness I could ascertain from experiencing other cultures that was unlike anything I could gain from reading a book or watching television. I commend my mom for allowing me to spread my wings and for advocating for me. I should mention that I created additional occasions for my mom to practice her advocacy for my travel. In college, I studied abroad in Ghana, England, Myanmar, and Thailand. By that point, my grandma had come around. She wasn't thrilled about all of these excursions, and yes, she still worried, but she accepted that I had gotten bitten by the travel bug. Now that I'm a parent, there are a whole host of atrocities that I can imagine at the thought of my own child being thousands and thousands of miles away. Yet with that, I am humbled by the ways in which my mom resisted the inclination to smother me with her fears, and instead gave me grace to grow.

A STRANGER IN MY HOUSE

*"I am a stranger, learning to love the
strangers around me."*
—June Jordan

Any time I hear the words "stranger in my house," my first
thought is of the song by R&B vocalist Tamia. She has an
incredibly beautiful voice. She is one of my favorite art-
ists! But the notion of living with a stranger also comes
to my mind when I think about child-rearing, especially when it comes to teenagers. I have heard parents and
parent-proxies lament about how "I don't know who he/
she is anymore." The adolescent period can be a particularly challenging time because parents of teenagers are
often acutely aware that at any given moment, both they
and their child are generating and sensing their feelings
about each other, whether they feel acceptance or resistance, whether they feel high or low tension, and whether
they feel support or confrontation. I am here to tell you
that, to a degree, this dynamic plays out with children of
all ages. I think it seems magnified in the teenage years
because of the teenager's ability to articulate, coupled

with developmentally appropriate assertions of independence. Yet despite the age of the child, at the heart of it all is the importance of the affective, or the feeling side, of parent-child relationships. The feelings are an important source of information—information about each individual's *real* concerns and what the possibilities are for establishing or maintaining a good relationship. What you preach to your kids—your rules, your advice—is equally as important as the interpersonal aspect of the relationship. There should be balance in the attention given to the *content* of your message and the *feelings* you are having about the interaction that is taking place as you convey the message.

There are four elements to the affective side of parent-child interactions that are always operating: responsibility, feelings, trust, and your own needs.

Responsibility

As far as responsibility goes, young children aside, each individual is responsible for how they engage, because the only person anyone ever truly has control over is themselves. So each individual is responsible for how they show up in the relationship.

Feelings

With regard to feelings, sometimes issues arise when there is questioning about the extent to which each individual is able to own their own feelings, as opposed to projecting their feelings onto someone else. While these concepts may seem beguiling to apply to parent-child relationships, I assure you that they are as relevant as they are in any other relationship.

Trust

The element of trust in the parent-child relationship boils down to boundaries and vulnerabilities. Male or female, young or old, everyone has boundaries of some sort. Everyone also has their own vulnerabilities. So recognize vulnerability. What do you do with it? Don't treat it like you'll have infinite chances to abuse it. Understand that the extent to which boundaries are respected and vulnerabilities safeguarded determines the level of trust that will be present.

Individual Needs

Every individual has a right to their own needs from the relationship. The need for acceptance, inclusion, and validation are human elements of any relationship.

CHAPTER 18

ON ELDERS AND THE VILLAGE VOICE

"Respect for your elders was one of the cornerstones of civilized behavior."
—Diana Gabaldon

The elders are an integral part of any village and should be cherished. Because experiences are as shaped by cultural background and life trajectories as they are by birth dates and generational divides, the presence of elders in our communities lends an unparalleled richness to the existence of us all. When members of our village grow older, it doesn't mean their voice or their stories are irrelevant. It means they have more stories to tell! Elders are how generations touch both the past and the future in the present. They can teach children things that members of younger generations simply cannot. They provide a sense of heritage and identity. They teach us about growing older and about how we age. They teach, through their living, what dying means. Elders can be a vital part of our understanding of what it is to be a human being—today, yesterday, and tomorrow. They are a repository of history. They can also be a wealth of wisdom and exemplars of resilience, because let's face it, getting old is not for the faint of heart. When I think about my elders, I realize that they survived the Great Depression, Jim Crow, the Civil Rights era, illness, ailments, and more than a handful of wars. When I think about my maternal grandparents specifically, I find it interesting that both Gramma and Gramps grew up without their mothers. I don't know how old either one of them was when their mothers died, nor do I know the cause of death, but I know that they and their siblings were raised by aunts. This is one of the many reasons why I like to acknowledge parent-proxies. What would have become of my grandparents if their aunts had not raised them well? What then would have become of me?

Of the many things that I learned from my elders, there are a few that I would like to share:

1) Slow down.

   If you live long enough to get old, Father Time will diminish your speed, your strength, and your sharpness. I imagine this is quite humbling. Circumstances force you to slow down. You become more reliant on others. And you grow in patience. What I learned is that moving through life at a different pace gives you a different view. Yet joy still finds you in the slower chapters. From spending lots of time with my grandparents and going at their pace, I learned to revel in slowing down.

2) Respect is important.

However, respect doesn't have to mean blind obedience, weak boundaries, undergoing abuse, or accepting that the elder is right by default. Instead, I take it to mean that you see the village elder, with their own set of unique experiences, as someone who has value and must be paid attention to and not taken for granted. To that end, I always found it particularly interesting to observe what the dynamic of respect looked like *between* the people that I loved and respected most—my parents and grandparents. Through that observation, I learned that giving respect to others requires self-control. I also saw that respect was considerate, courteous, and inclusive.

3) It's okay to tell it like it is.

I don't know about you, but most of the elders I know don't sugarcoat a thing! Yet, miraculously, they can deliver with a warm candor that I find refreshing, and often amusing. Tact and candor can co-exist, but when they don't, the world won't crumble. So say what you have to say. Don't mince words.

4) Take care of what you have.

   Through their example, I learned to take pride in the way you take care of things. And very simply, new isn't always better, and quantity isn't always better than quality.

Other members of the village are valuable as well. When I say "village," I think of people I can trust. I think of people who have similar values, yet are different enough to challenge me and help me grow. I think of people that can stand in the gap. I think of people that can, for instance, offer my child the same principles I uphold, but with a different voice. Moreover, the village should be a space where you can be open to meaningful feedback. You need people that will tell you what you don't want to but need to hear and will love you through it. I think of checks and balances. I think of safety and support and uplifting. And this type of architecture, in its entirety, is something I think we can all benefit from. Your tribe determines your vibe, and vice versa.

CHAPTER 19

ON DISAGREEMENTS

"Communication is not the key to a successful relationship, comprehension is. Common understanding is the key to connection."

—Unknown

Disagreements. They will happen. Disagreements are a lack of alignment of one person's needs with the needs of another person. If two people have unmet needs that are incongruous, then there is discord. But if you can more quickly take responsibility for your actions, repair can come more quickly. Sure, it feels great when you vibe with someone and you are both on the same page, but usually when people disagree, it's not the subject of the disagreement that is most bothersome. Often, it's the *way* that the person disagrees. So, there's what happened. Then, there's the content beneath what happened.

When there is a power dynamic as there is in a typical parent-child relationship, it is not uncommon for the child to feel as if they don't matter or don't have a voice. Parental disagreements can embody a sentiment of, "I'm the adult and I get to do what I want anyway," or "My feelings are more important than yours right now," or "What others think of me is more important than you."

I remind parents that when you want to understand where someone else is coming from, there's a certain way you communicate. Thinking about the other person's feelings crafts how you talk to them. I also encourage parents not to take disagreements with their children as disrespect. If we're lucky, we raise bright, critical thinkers that can take on the world. That type of child is not one that always acquiesces.

It is human nature to want to be right. (Your kids are human, too, by the way.) However, sometimes it's not about having the right solution—it's about simply witnessing the other person. The desire to be right is the ego. It gets in the way of having transformative conversations. Our ego thinks that others should take us into consideration. Our ego does not want to be criticized. Our ego wants to be acknowledged. So if your ego takes over, you're in a constant struggle with the rest of the world. It drains your energy. It is far easier to not take things personally. You experience more harmony and connection. So sometimes (emphasis on *sometimes)*, it boils down to the question—do you want to be happy or do you want to be right?

Admittedly, I hate this dichotomy. And you may be wondering, how is this applicable to child-rearing? Why would you not take things personally when they take place within one of your most personal relationships, the relationship with your child? Well, I think it is particularly important when considering relationships with toddlers and teenagers. What's at the root of harmony with these particular age groups, which represent loads of self-discovery and an assertion of independence, is the value in seeing their perspectives. It's not about you. Shift your focus from "me" to "we." When you shift your focus from one to the other, you *make space for* understanding instead of irritation. There's a flip side to every coin. Look at the other person's intention. However, *that* requires discipline and intention on your part. Parenting is a mental marathon. But know that your day-to-day dealings are imparting wisdom and life skills to your child.

I believe that disagreements do not have to lead to disunion. But I also believe that there can be damage done by what's spoken. There can be damage done by behavior. And there can be damage done by what's unspoken. Silence is not always peace. Sometimes, children will tolerate your dysfunction out of necessity, or because of the perks that come with being with you. Which means, there will come a point at which they may choose to tolerate it no more. What I need parents to understand is that it is a human response to distance oneself from people and situations that make you feel hurt, unimportant, and disempowered—whether it's physical distance, proverbial walls, or new behaviors. What I have found interesting is that children are often expected to display resiliency, compassion, and forgiveness in the name of adult comfort, while acting as a balm for the very person that did not prioritize them, that suppressed their perspective out of convenience, and robbed them of their humanity. In some neurological research, it is found that when people's dignity is harmed, it produces the same response in the brain as a physical injury. Be that as it may, I do not believe that disagreements have to be undignified. So I encourage parents to take into account the desired outcome. *Reaction* happens without thought or intention. (If you haven't noticed by now, I'm all about intention.) Reaction is grounded in our survival instincts. *Response* is a little different. Response is considerate and solution-oriented. You have the power to choose whether you react or respond. Know also that there is tremendous power in repair after there has been a rupture in relationship. There is power in apology. There is power in self-awareness.

CHAPTER 20

ON DISCIPLINE

"All kids need love. All kids need limits."
—Unknown

Here's my prevailing thought on discipline: I do not believe in abusing children in the name of discipline. The word "discipline" comes from the word "disciple." A disciple is not someone who is afraid of you, but someone who loves you and wants to belong to you. Discipline is teaching in disguise, not fear.

Discipline is also several other things. Discipline is direction. Discipline is decorum. Discipline is safety. Discipline is boundaries. Discipline is structure. According to psychologist Dr. Jordan B. Peterson, discipline means not being defeated by your own impulses. With all of that said, I do believe that children require discipline. *Require.* But no discipline is enjoyable while it's happening. For parents that struggle with enforcing discipline, I offer you some thoughtful words from author, educator, and founder of Capital Preparatory Schools, Dr. Steve Perry: "The discomfort of watching your child be unhappy mustn't be greater than the benefit of them being corrected." If you discipline someone properly, they become disciplined. That means they are competent in being able to master their own impulses.

Dealing with tantrums, tensions, and tears is challenging. Not infrequently, cycles of misbehavior receive the punitive punctuation of deprivation and punishment. This is because situations that require discipline are not infrequently centered around the defiance of authority.

Yet, situations that require discipline are really opportunities for growth. They are opportunities to achieve empathy, insight, and repair. At the heart of disciplinary challenges, there is uncertainty about what the best methods are to communicate the lessons you are trying to impart. At the heart of it, there is uncertainty about how to communicate in a constructive way about your concerns, your frustrations, and your solutions.

In her book titled *Out of Control: Why Disciplining Your Child Doesn't Work and What Will*, clinical psychologist Dr. Shefali Tsabary suggests that it is the dynamic that arises from insisting on our parental agenda that creates the need for discipline. She goes on to say that when discipline focuses on behavior and not on the feelings driving the behavior, it undercuts the very thing we are trying to accomplish. If, instead, a parent or parent-proxy puts out the kind of vibes that welcome feelings, even when the feelings are difficult to tolerate, the child picks up on this and eventually learns how to manage their feelings in a healthy manner. As a pediatrician, I believe there are all kinds of ways we can help our children cope with their world. Further, I understand that explorative rule-breaking, for instance, is a normal part of development. Yet as the mother of a black boy in particular, being open to all kinds of ways to help him cope with the world and teach him to be disciplined is not something I take lightly. It is my hope that I am able to discipline him in a way that respects his personhood and prepares him for the world, without thwarting his curiosity, independence, and confidence.

My objective here is to challenge our thinking regarding the way that we conceptualize discipline. Discipline is necessary, but I recognize that discipline is also a major cause of generations of dysfunction. The patterns of behavior we witness in childhood become the template for our own way of parenting. Children learn from how we relate to them. So if we are to *transform lives for generations*, we must critically examine our approach to discipline and how we are choosing to relate to our children. As far as specific disciplinary techniques go, that needs to be a more nuanced discussion to be most effective because it requires consideration for who your child is and how your child is. It's about teaching who you have in a way that registers, and not necessarily about teaching within your realm of comfort. When children are taught why certain actions are expected and others are prohibited, they internalize reasons for these behaviors. As a result, their motivation to behave properly comes from within. They are more likely to engage in expected behaviors when they are not being watched. When children conform to expectations to avoid punishment, love withdrawal, or abandonment, their motivation to behave appropriately is external. Thus, discipline is fleeting.

Generally speaking, the best discipline is a mixture of nurturing, firmness, structure, limit-setting, receptiveness, accountability, persistence, empathy, and assertion of authority. I do recommend that parents and parent-proxies employ elements of different disciplinary styles to varying degrees in relation to particular aspects of life, such as household responsibilities, rule enforcement, environmental setting, village support availability, and the like. I also recommend that parents and parent-proxies do not withhold expectations, but instead are clear and consistent with expectations. Communicate that your child is capable of meeting the demands that life places on him/her. Then set reasonable consequences when a limit has been breached.

The most important discipline in the home, however, is a parent's own self-discipline. It is the ability to step away when anger flares, remain calm in times of crisis, and hold compassion and rationality when a child struggles. But discipline is hard to find if you are feeling more broken than whole.

CHAPTER 21

ON EMOTIONS

"Feelings are much like waves. We can't stop them from coming, but we can choose which one to surf."

—Jonatan Mårtensson

The limbic system of the brain is responsible for how we process and experience emotions. Being able to feel emotions is part of what makes us human. Emotions are motivating. Emotions give meaning to experience. Yet many people struggle to understand their emotions and the things that cause us to feel so deeply. Emotionally, we often experience a huge range of different things in response to any situation. Positive emotions are meant to reinforce an experience as enjoyable so that we seek it out again. We seek positive emotions such as pleasure, calm, excitement, interest, and joy. They activate the reward systems within the brain that make us feel safe. Negative emotions, on the other hand, warn us of potentially dangerous situations and raise the survival instincts within us so that we become much more aware. We avoid negative emotions such as fear, anxiety, pain, embarrassment, and shame. However, we are constantly experiencing new things, which means our emotions are rarely static, which complicates being able to identify what is going on with our emotions. It is important that we as parents and parent-proxies identify our emotions deliberately. It helps us help our children to develop their emotional vocabulary.

According to psychologist Dr. Robert Plutchick, there are eight basic emotions that are at the core of our experiences, reactions, and sensations. They are: anger, sadness, fear, joy, anticipation, surprise, disgust, and shame. There is no consensus about the precise number of basic emotions, but combinations of basic emotions will produce new, complex emotions. These are sometimes depicted in a Feelings Wheel which shows the range of human emotions and how they relate to one another. Whether visual depiction or mere conceptualization suits your fancy, the benefits of this kind of identification are myriad. Being able to highly differentiate one's own emotions in a flexible way can help you to regulate your emotions more effectively. In others, being able to better distinguish the intensity of emotions and utilize a greater emotional vocabulary is a sign of heightened emotional intelligence and typically allows more specific communication around feelings and enhanced relational satisfaction.

Before we delve deeper into this conversation on emotions, we must acknowledge the performative wellness that is asked of many children at one time or another. It sounds like, "Wipe that look off your face," or "Stop whining, you're okay," when they are clearly expressing that they are not okay; or it sounds like, "If you don't stop crying, I'll give you something to cry about." These types of reactions do not help children to foster emotional regulation. It teaches them to suppress, perform, and people-please. We must not deny children of their emotional experience. It deprives them of the opportunity to gain acceptance of their difficult feelings. Instead, to the whining child, you can say, "It's hard to understand you when you whine. Let's try to talk when you're ready." Acknowledge. Create space. Children should have the freedom to experience and express all of their emotions without being told that it's not acceptable. This is of monumental importance. Because part of my clinical practice includes screening for and counseling around substance use in adolescents, what I've come to realize is this—people don't become addicted to drugs or alcohol, but rather, they become addicted to escaping reality. Therefore, one of the best things I can do for my child in addition to creating space for the full breadth of his emotions, is to teach him skills to help him confront and cope with his emotions in honest, healthy, and nondestructive ways. Further, I contend that biology is inseparable from our psychological dynamics and social relationships.

In a fascinating book titled, *The Body Keeps the Score: Brain, Mind, and Body in the Healing of Trauma*, author Bessel van der Kolk exposes the tremendous power of our relationships to both hurt and heal, while also acknowledging the importance of mental and emotional factors in the causation of illness—not just physiological ones. Therefore, when I make my child's whole wellbeing my business, that means that there is space for the entirety of him and what he feels.

Something that I find helpful for parents to understand about their children, and about themselves, is the concept of primary emotions and secondary emotions. Differentiating between primary and secondary emotions provides powerful coping skills, and coping skills are important for children and adults alike. Moreover, I think the ability to distinguish primary and secondary emotions also provides insight into behaviors. Primary emotions are fairly simple to understand. They are your reactions to external events. Primary emotions are "fast-acting." That is, they occur in close proximity to the event that brought them on. Primary emotions are important because they provide us with information about our current situation and get us ready or motivated to act in some way.

A secondary emotion is when you feel something about the feeling itself. Secondary emotions turn emotions into complex reactions. They increase the intensity of your reactions. Secondary emotions tend to stick around for a long time. They are also problematic because they can "take over" from primary emotions, effectively blocking them. As a result, secondary emotions can keep you from getting information from your primary emotions and acting on it in healthy ways. You could think of this as a way of trying to avoid your emotions.

Secondary emotions can also be classified into instrumental emotions. These are unconscious and habitual. Instrumental emotions are attempts to manipulate the environment. Crying to avoid expected punishment is an example of an instrumental emotion. We learn instrumental emotions as children as a form of conditioning. For example, when we cry, a parent comes to soothe us, so we learn to use the facial expressions and response associated with crying when we need that soothing or sense of security. Many toddlers are very adept at using instrumental emotions to get their way with anger. A toddler throws a tantrum, and parents give in to make them quiet. As we get older, we learn that this behavior is not appropriate; if not, we become spoiled and manipulative. By not learning the correct secondary emotional response, it leaves the person distant and emotionally detached from those around them. However, a child who has a secure relationship with a parent learns to regulate emotions under stress and in difficult situations.

Another reason why identifying emotions is important is to be able to react to them properly. Finding the real cause behind a person's reaction means examining the primary emotion. The secondary emotion will help you to understand how that person processes information. It is also worth noting that, beginning in childhood, what we experience becomes organized into "emotion schemes." Emotion schemes are formed when emotions are connected to memories of the self in the situation. Emotion schemes include bodily sensations, symbolic representations, and action tendencies. As a result, the emotional reaction can be recreated again and again long after the event. Then a reminder of a painful event, such as a betrayal for instance, can stimulate an emotional reaction. As I'm sure you can imagine, parents and parent-proxies have a crucial role in supporting and responding to their children's emotional needs.

CHAPTER 22

ON PERSONALITY AND ATTACHMENT TYPE

"Learn the difference between connection and attachment. Connection gives you power, attachment sucks the life out of you."

—Unknown

One of the most exciting things for me as a pediatrician is watching the personality of babies blossom over time as they mature. I'm sure it is an excitement that all parents can identify with. I consider myself blessed to witness it over and over through other people's children. It is interesting because children come into this world like blank slates. As they grow, so do their personalities. Personality development begins with the biological foundations of temperament and over time becomes increasingly elaborated, extended, and refined. Yet personality is made up of many other features besides temperament. Personality influences the type of relationships that children will attract and be attracted to. But parents also influence the type of relationships that their children will attract and be attracted to. Parental relationships directly influence the protective mechanisms that your child will develop that ultimately determine the types of relationships they establish with others. The ability to form attachments with other human beings is an essential skill that typically begins early in life. The parent/caregiver-child relationship is the first crucial relationship that an infant forms, and the health of this relationship has a profound effect on the child's social and emotional development. Attachment theory provides a model for understanding development within the context of the child's primary and formative relationships, and also provides a model for understanding an adult's orientation toward lifelong intimate connections, social and romantic relationships, as well as independent exploration. The four attachment types are as follows:

- **Secure attachment** – Formed when a parent/parent-proxy responds consistently with care, comfort, and devoted attention. This child trusts and relies upon their caregiver's presence and is calmed by them.

- **Avoidant attachment** – Formed when a parent/parent-proxy is dismissive toward their child's distress or is responsive only to their physical needs and does not provide emotional comfort. This child is less likely to seek comfort from their caregiver.

- **Anxious attachment** – Formed when a parent/parent-proxy responds with comfort in some instances, but is absent or annoyed in others. This child's reactions to their caregiver are equally inconsistent.

- **Disorganized attachment** – Formed when a parent/parent-proxy neglects their child or has them in an environment of turbulence, fear, and instability. This child's behavior won't change whether their caregiver is there or not, but it may be marked by unpredictable or intense reactions.

The benefits of a secure attachment include autonomy, successful interactions with peers, less conflict with parents, less aggression, less anxiety, and willingness to explore. Children who form secure relationships are overall more socially competent. Children who form secure relationships with their parent/parent-proxy have fewer internalizing and externalizing behaviors. An internalizing behavior is a behavior directed inwardly toward oneself. It is an over-controlled, neurotic, and self-directed type of behavior. Internalizing behaviors can include eating disorders, substance abuse, anxiety disorders, depressive disorders, selective mutism, social withdrawal, and self-harm. Some risk factors for internalizing behavior are family conflict, parental rejection, lack of parental warmth, sexual abuse, and childhood neglect.

Externalizing behavior is behavior directed outwardly toward others or the social environment. It is characterized as an under-controlled, delinquent, and out-directed mode of responding. Examples of externalizing behaviors include physical aggression, relational aggression, hyperactivity, disruptiveness, defiance, theft, and vandalism. Risk factors for externalizing behavior can include parental substance abuse, poverty, and situations of high psychosocial stress such as divorce, prolonged illness, housing insecurity, and death. Of note, a child may have internalizing behavior and externalizing behavior at the same time.

Any attachment style that is not secure attachment falls under the umbrella of insecure attachment—the three types of which have previously been listed. Insecure attachment is collectively characterized by the lack of or the distortion of mutuality in relationships. Children with attachment disorders exhibit a varying capacity to form and sustain relationships and demonstrate emotional depth, and they tend to experience a higher level of peer conflict. Additionally, children with insecure attachments have a greater likelihood for physical health morbidities and impaired social, neurobiological, and psychological functioning that extends into adulthood.

In adulthood, those with secure attachments tend to have supportive and communicative relationships. Secure attachment is integral to a healthy life. However, keep in mind that people are not always just one attachment style. Each style exists on a spectrum. Also note that we all have multiple experiences that influence our ability to form healthy relationships over time. Yet by overcoming core wounds, we can all work toward being secure in our relationships.

CHAPTER 23

ON ADULT CHILDREN

"Each moment with our child is a reflection of the past and a foundation for the future."
—Shefali Tsabary

A healthy parent-child relationship is the result of the efforts that both parties put in, and neither of them should be burdened with this responsibility alone. I want to take a brief opportunity here to talk about maintaining relationships with adult children, because I find it unfortunate when relational closeness is sacrificed at the expense of comfort. Sometimes, relationships with adult children are challenging when the parents exhibit difficulty in accepting their children as adults. Perhaps it is rooted in a parental longing for more time to "get it right" before your child slips through your grasp. Or it could be related to the assertion of independence that comes with adulthood, which often shifts how the power dynamic manifests, along with shifting perceptions of what it means to be "respectful." Sometimes relationships with adult children are challenging because one person is stuck in the old version of the relationship, and that version does not support the vision that the other person has for their life. Essentially, we outgrow those that do not know how to love us in a way that we can receive—in a way that resonates and fulfills our needs. In my experience, what I have also realized is that sometimes parents hate what they inadvertently taught their children, so being close to them becomes a painful reminder of their perceived failure. In that case, being distant or playing pretend is far easier than the acknowledgment of unspoken shame, disappointment, or of shortcomings that require courage to give a voice to. Sometimes, there is strain on the parent-adult child relationship because there is the expectation that love and care be demonstrated as the upholding of wrongdoing, to which one party does not ascribe.

Other times, I have found that discord between adult children and their parents is centered around what is perceived to be the truth. Dissimilar recounts of history regarding a shared experience can be quite difficult to contend with. Parents sometimes don't do things that children feel like they're supposed to do. Or parents behave in a way that leaves their children thinking, "How could their choices not include me?" To that, I will say this—no one holds a monopoly on "truth." It is a matter of perspective. Representations of truth come about through the recognition that different people can each hold different pieces of truth. Better representations of truth can come about by the mixture and integration of different ideas from different people. Yet even when grievances aren't extreme, I know that unresolved hurts between you and your parents can show up in your parenting. This is where an awareness for generational wellness comes into play. This is also a good place to mention reconciliation and resolution. They are two different concepts. If you place your healing on reconciliation, then you may struggle til the day you die. Reconciliation means acknowledging hurtful actions and their resulting emotions, then apologizing for one's part in an issue, forgiving, and letting go of associated grudges. Reconciliation takes two people. But you can't make another person come to the table to reconcile. Resolution, however, just takes one person. You can always decide what you will or will not participate in, or how you will participate in it. You can resolve to move forward without someone else's permission.

Discord between adult children and their parents can also be rooted in unmet expectations that, on either side, have added up over time and created resentment. Here, I think it useful to cite journalist Joshua David Stein's perspective on love as he related it to his school-aged son through the analogy of a math problem.

$$
\begin{array}{r}
6 \\
+ 3 \\
\hline
\end{array}
$$

"What I want to say about love has to do with the line, not the operation above it. It has to do with the very natural impulse to draw it at all . . . It enacts the action . . . Love means never drawing that line. Love makes calculation impossible . . . In other words, there's no total; there's just the numbers, moments, values. Some are positive (addition) and some are negative (subtraction). Some operations within a relationship multiply and some divide. Those are its functions. But love lives as long as the equation isn't totaled."

So, love exists in holding open the opportunity for change. In that same space, there can be the opportunity for repair, for resolution, and for growth in love, no matter the age. Ultimately, these adult relationships can be maintained when both sides are willing to expand their sphere of comfortable action.

CHAPTER 24

GRIEVING PARENTS

"Grief is like the ocean: it comes on in waves, ebbing and flowing. Sometimes the water is calm, and sometimes it is overwhelming. All we can do is learn to swim."

—Vicki Harrison

One night I fell asleep on the couch in my basement. The following morning after I eased into waking, I heard the pitter-patter of busy feet running downstairs. My son and my husband came to the basement to deliver a morning greeting . . . and to watch basketball highlights on the big screen TV. Then my five-year-old crawled onto the couch on top of me to give me a hug. He sweetly said, "Good morning, Mommy," and gave me a kiss on my cheek. Our hug lingered into an easy cuddle, and I found myself slipping into that place of sweet, pure joy that I know only because of him. It's special. It's tender. My face settled perfectly into the nook of his neck. I breathed him in, and the side of my face became his pillow, my body his mattress, his little hands gently splayed in my hair. As he watched basketball, I mentally planned my day. Amidst the planning, I stepped back into the present and thought, "I just love these moments. I never want to be here without him." Yes. Here. As in, on this earth. As in, in existence. Now why did I think that?! I don't know. Sometimes my mind goes to places that I don't like. Thinking of the unfathomable. Thinking of my deepest fear. The heaviness of my brown skin and his brown skin and what that means to certain members of society came into play. I shook it off. I didn't want the tendrils of racism to taint our beautiful moment. So I no longer viewed our potential separation through that lens, but my mind was still on the "What if?" Not the "What if he got killed?" thought, but I was still wondering, "What if something else happened?" The void is unimaginable.

Though racial violence and injustice is not a reality for all parents, I think all parents worry in a similar way, at least to some degree. We all know that, try as we might, we can't protect our children from everything. I then realized that my spirit was carrying the sorrow of an acquaintance who lost her adult son just a couple of weeks prior. No matter how old, they're always our babies, and it's always unnatural for them to leave this world before we do. So my heart hurt for that mom . . . and for all the parents who know what it is to experience the death of a child.

Of the bonds formed within the family, the parent-child bond is not only particularly strong, but also integral to the identity of many parents and children. Much has been written about the significance of the parent-child bond as a major organizer of an individual's positive sense of self and its significance as it applies to relationships with others. As you can imagine, this bond changes greatly with bereavement, making it a particularly complex and dynamic process that does not necessarily proceed in an orderly, linear fashion. For miscarriages, stillbirths, and newborn deaths, there's not just the death of the child, but there's the death of the excitement for the little person you didn't get the opportunity to know. For the death of infants and older children (at whatever age), there's the death of the child, the death of the possibilities you had for them, and the death of those beloved, reciprocal interactions. In any case, the pain of grief is extremely intense as parents digest the finality of not seeing their child.

According to data from the Centers for Disease Control and Prevention (CDC) as well as the American Academy of Pediatrics (AAP), about half of all child deaths occur during infancy, most with limited preparation time. Unintentional injuries are the leading cause of death in children ages one to fourteen and account for more than half of all deaths among young people ages fifteen to nineteen. Serious unintentional injuries result from a myriad of causes, including motor vehicle crashes, falls, burns, poisoning, drowning, firearms, recreational activities, prescription or other drug overdose, and sports. In addition, while the overall death rate for children aged fourteen and younger has declined substantially since the 1950s, deaths from intentional injuries have been on the rise. Childhood homicide rates have tripled, and suicide rates have quadrupled since then.

A child's death causes a profound family crisis. Integrating the loss of a child into the life narrative and making sense and new meanings of such a wrenching event present a challenge to parents, parent-proxies, and other loved ones. Nothing prepares one for the loss of a child, whether sudden or expected. Facing such a devastating reality has multiple meanings for everyone involved. There are many reverberations that occur as a consequence of adjusting to loss. Some relationships with family and friends are strengthened, others are found wanting. Bereaved individuals have reported their experience of having changed as a result of the loss, of learning to value anew what is really important to them and as a result of reviewing priorities. Grief impacts a parent's whole identity as well as the identity and security of other members of the family. The ways in which feelings and emotions of grief are experienced and expressed differ from person to person. Some emotions of grief can be shared, while other intense feelings may never be put into words. The death of a child isn't something you get over. It is something you learn to live with. In time, the pain of loss, although always there, becomes less intensive. The parent-child relationship often takes on new forms as a parent connects with their child in new ways. The love you have for your child is not severed, but rather, your relationship continues in a different context.

The death of a child is perhaps one of the most difficult and penetrating experiences for surviving siblings, grandparents, parent-proxies, and other family members as well as parents. Parents' management of their own grief has an enormous impact on their surviving children. One of the main challenges confronting the adults is how to explain death to their surviving children. Developmental attributes are likely to influence how siblings experience and express their loss. For example, young children are more likely to harbor unrealistic fears of their own vulnerability to the illness, injuries, or condition their sibling experienced. Adolescents are more vulnerable to depression in response to the parents' grief and subsequent withdrawal from them as the adolescent goes through normal separation from the family. Parents may sometimes become distressed because it appears to them that the siblings have adjusted too quickly, grieved too little, or appeared totally unaffected by the death. Parents may have a difficult time coping with the behavioral changes, demands, and needs of the siblings as they are absorbed in their own grief and have little energy to extend beyond themselves. It is important that siblings don't become the "forgotten grievers."

All children who experience a significant death in their family, or among friends, need parents or another adult who will tell them the truth about the death in simple, understandable terms, and who will listen to their questions and concerns.

Children of all ages can benefit from the validation of the normalcy and appropriateness of a broad range of grief reactions to the death of a sibling. They need frequent reassurance of your love and understanding. They can also benefit from the conscious provision of opportunities for them to talk, when ready. Further, recognition of their unique relationship to the sibling and their individual responses to the loss of that relationship within their personal and familial situation is key.

Here, I think it is important to reiterate that it takes a village to raise a child. But also, it takes a village to traverse this journey called life. For those parents and parent-proxies who have experienced the death of a child, I encourage you to empower a broad range of support systems as you navigate this journey.

As a physician, I have occasionally delivered such horrible news, or have witnessed the last breaths of a child as their family did the same. I've heard the shrill, agonizing cry that accompanies that moment. I've cried with them. I've held shaky, sweaty hands. I've seen parents collapse with grief as some of their life is taken away the moment that their child ceases to live. All that said, nobody wants to be brave. Bravery is what you do when you don't have any more choices. I know that it takes bravery to face the world without a piece of you. So for those to whom this applies—I'm sorry. I see you. My heart goes out to you.

PART II P3Q's

- What does your child learning about themself look like in your presence? Do your interactions with your child strip them of their sense of self?

- Do your kids know who you are outside of your role as their parent? Do they have a relationship with who you are? Do YOU know who you are outside of your parenting role?

- How are you responding to and rebounding from challenges that you have with your kids?

- Have you made space in your life for someone else to give you counsel?

- How do you react when you know your child feels hurt? Are you capable of expressions of empathy when you are hurt at the same time?

- Do the goals you have for your children and for your parenting align with how you choose to discipline?

PART III:
THE FOUNDATION

CHAPTER 25

DON'T WAKE DADDY

"Knowing is not enough. We must apply.
Willing is not enough. We must do."
—Johann Wolfgang von Goethe

I'm probably dating myself, but when I was a kid, I remember a commercial for a game called Don't Wake Daddy. It was a board game created by Parker Brothers in which players took the role of children sneaking to the refrigerator late at night, trying not to wake their sleeping father who lies in the middle of the board on a large bed. It's funny; even now as I type, I can hear that commercial play in my head. In any case, now being a mom, the title of this game got me thinking—specifically about how in partnerships, especially parenting, each party usually feels that there is an unequal division of labor. Parenting is a labor of love, but a labor nonetheless.

There is a brilliant article written by Melissa Hogenboom for BBC titled, *"The hidden load: How 'thinking of everything' holds mums back."* It touches on what I like to call the inherent maintenance of comfort and protection for men. Numerous studies show that women in heterosexual relationships still do the bulk of housework and childcare. Many couples aim to split their responsibilities fifty-fifty, yet for various structural and socio-economic reasons, couples end up allocating tasks along typically gendered lines, even in an otherwise progressive relationship where both the woman and the man bring home the bacon and fry it up in a pan. Even in couples who think that they have achieved an equal division of labor, the more hidden forms of care generally end up falling to the woman. Women are much more likely than men to report that the division of childcare with their spouses is imbalanced, perhaps because, as one study found, men perceive that they are doing their fair share when they contribute to just 36 percent of the work at home.

Experts say that this hidden work comes in three overlapping categories. First, there's cognitive labor—which is thinking about all the practical elements of household responsibilities, including organizing playdates, meal planning, managing doctor's appointments, and planning activities. Second, there's emotional labor—which is maintaining the family's emotions. This can look like calming things down if the kids are acting up, being the one to consistently model emotional regulation, worrying about how they are managing at school, or investing the effort to maintain healthy relationships with family and friends. Third is the mental load, which is the intersection of the two. This includes preparing, organizing, and anticipating everything—emotional and practical—that needs to get done to make life flow. Even when both partners are hands-on parents, moms still handle more of the "mental load." This hidden work is hard to measure because it's invisible and performed internally, making it difficult to know where it starts and ends.

Our strengths, unrecognized, unappreciated, and out of balance, become a source of frustration. It is important to note that this imbalance presents several risks. One risk is the exhaustion of the partner who doesn't benefit from the imbalance, who might initially ask for help and could come across as nagging if they have to repeat themselves again and again. That then wears on relationships. According to University of Utah sociologist Daniel Carlson, an unequal distribution of caring responsibilities in couples can also lead to less sex. I'm sure that raised some eyebrows! A third risk is that when women in particular are over-stretched at home, they may feel physically or mentally unable to put in the extra hours demanded by many workplaces, so the gender pay gap continues to widen. This affects the entire household. With all of that said, I do want to note that same-sex couples also struggle to find the balance.

When labor is divided unevenly, there are also risks posed to the children. Here's how: Children are constantly observing the world—mainly, studying people and their differences—and making inferences based on what they see and hear about these differences. They start to discern the power discrepancy. According to psychologist Darcy Lockman, this finding is a testament to kids' ability to identify implicit power, to parse whose personhood is more valuable, and to discern whose beliefs are more important and therefore worth adopting as their own. This all ties in to how they treat you, who they will become, and how well they will develop collaborative and cooperative social relationships.

A growing body of research in family and clinical studies demonstrates that spousal equality promotes marital success, and that inequality undermines it. When the disparity is gendered, it perpetuates attitudes about what is and should be acceptable—or even desirable—between a woman and a man, with children as an eager audience. Various studies show that, among heterosexual parents, fathers—even the youngest and most theoretically progressive among them—do not partake *generously* of the workload at home. Employed women partnered with employed men carry 65 percent of the family's childcare responsibilities, a figure that has held steady since the turn of the century. Women with babies enjoy half as much leisure time on weekends as their husbands. Working mothers with preschool-age children are 2.5 times as likely to perform middle-of-the-night care as their husbands. And in hours not so easily tallied, mothers remain almost solely in charge of the endless managerial care that comes with raising children: securing babysitters, filling out school forms, remembering schedules, sorting through hand-me-downs.

What I know is that men's attitudes about marital roles, not women's, are ultimately internalized by both their daughters and their sons. What we also know is that sexism starts in childhood. However, it can also be stopped there. But only if parents push a stronger message than our culture does.

From my experience coaching parents, I can tell you that while awareness, acknowledgement, and appreciation can be a salve to the injury created with this unequal division of labor, the real cure is to enact behaviors that prevent reinjury. In order to foster new habits to help share the load, you must first accept that you will do things differently. You must also be willing to do things differently without resentment. Ideals are no substitute for behavior. Know that there is emotional labor involved in doing the work, but there is also emotional labor connected to a decision *not* to do a task. Be mindful of that as well. Additionally, we must make the invisible more visible. Each person in the partnership also needs to be honest about their strengths and priorities. Communicate often. And finally, make peace with your choices.

CHAPTER 26

IT'S ONLY MONDAY MORNING AND I'M ALREADY TIRED

"You can fail at plenty as long as you get a few important things right."

—Tim Ferris

All parents know that being tired during the era before kids (BK) and being tired in the era after kids (AK) are *completely* different! Since starting my journey in motherhood, there have been times when I have been so tired that I felt like I would never be untired again. There have been times when I've felt like there wasn't enough of me to do all that I wanted and needed to do. Both of these are simply horrible feelings. Quiet as it's kept, many parents have moments when they feel like they have nothing left, when they wish the kids didn't need them quite so much, or when they need a break but aren't able to take it. A sentiment that I think resonates with all parents is the feeling that there simply are not enough hours in the day, or that there's not enough of you to go around. Maybe this feeling is brought on by mental overload. Maybe it's from physical fatigue. Maybe it's emotional drain. Maybe it's feeling defeated. Or maybe it's the exhaustion that comes from being a constant example. A particularly taxing form of parental fatigue is the kind that leaves you feeling disempowered and unable to easily see a solution. Whatever form it takes, it's horrible.

The levels of exhaustion I have experienced have caused me to question how I show up—for my kid, for the world. Admittedly, I wasn't always happy with the answer. However, I have come to accept that the way my best looks varies from day to day. And sometimes, I can't even say that I'm giving my best. Yet often, it's good enough. It may not be ideal, and all of the boxes might not be checked, but it's good enough. The overachiever in me initially bristled at this notion, but usually, my kid is okay! So if he's okay, I can learn to be okay—with the situation, and with me. I have also learned that at times like these, your village is particularly important. Whether it's a friend that can come over to watch the baby so you can take a nap, or an uncle to take the kids to the playground so you can get work done without interruptions, it's times like this when you should rely on your village. And it is worth explicitly stating that there are times when you will need more than a few hours to do some semblance of a recharge. That's okay too. Use your village and allow yourself to be comforted and cared for. Sometimes you have to make you a priority so that you can make them (your kids) a priority. (More on that in the next chapter.)

Parenthood requires you to be intentional with your time and attention, both of which are finite resources. What I have come to develop an intimate understanding of is that time and bandwidth are two different things. Just because I have the time to do something doesn't mean I have the bandwidth to do it. Managing my *energy* as well as my *time* is a crucial lesson I have learned as a parent. A certain level of multitasking is inevitable as a parent, because, let's face it, life sometimes requires us to switch focus to and from many different things quickly without allowing extended periods of adjustment when making the switch. We have to recurrently juggle priorities, combined with the thinking that we aren't able to spend as much time as we want on any one task, or that we aren't giving our children the support they really need because no matter how much we do, we're never catching up. All this switching is not only stressful, but studies have also shown that there are inefficiencies to frequent change. Ultimately, my well-being comes down to balancing what I need and what is needed from me in the current time.

Speaking of time, so many of us live for the weekends. We try to survive the weekdays, which are usually comprised of whatever it is we do to make a living on top of handling the kids' schooling and all that it entails—waking up early, making breakfast, packing lunch, drop-off, pickup, chauffeuring to extracurricular activities, reviewing or helping with homework, making dinner, then bath time and tuck-in. After all of that, maybe we have a little bit left in us to give to our partner or watch our favorite sitcom. With all of that, the weekend gets placed on a pedestal because there aren't quite as many moving parts to worry about. Weekends seem like a vacation. But not really. The juggle struggle is *real*. And Monday always comes around again too soon. The way that we manage this depends on our own unique circumstances. Regardless of what those circumstances may be, it is our personal responsibility to be as balanced as possible in order to consistently offer love and practice presence. It is inevitable that parents will encounter stress and exhaustion during the process of raising their children, but it is up to each of us to care for ourselves so that we may best care for our families. I just encourage you to remember that time and bandwidth are two different things. I repeat—time and bandwidth are two different things. If you manage your bandwidth, time will follow.

CHAPTER 27

SELF-CARE

Take a break or break.

Becoming a parent can be lonely and isolating. If you aren't careful, life with kids can swallow you up completely. As such, self-care is necessary. In recent years, the term "self-care" has become trite, but its importance is still great as ever. It is easy to fall into a service mentality as a parent. You see yourself charged with solving your child's problems and serving their needs—and it is possible to act in such a way that you appear not to have any needs of your own. The reality is that you do have needs. You need to rest. You need to nourish your body. You need to nourish your mind. You need to nourish your spirit. You need to vent. Part of parenting is sacrifice, but you should not always be an afterthought. Occasionally retreating from your world for contemplation, meditation, purification, and renewal is both healthy and necessary. Yet sometimes it's like we need permission to take care of ourselves. Well, here it is: *take care of you.* Putting yourself first does not have to mean that you are selfish. Not all self-interested behavior is selfish. Exercising a lack of consideration is selfish. Reclaiming your identity that exists outside of parenthood is not selfish. In fact, it is imperative that you maintain some of your identities that are about your relationship with yourself as opposed to investing all of your energy into the identities that are about your relationship to someone else. You matter. Doing something purely for your enjoyment and yours alone is not selfish. So you have my blessing and my encouragement to do you.

Routine self-care is not only essential for you but also for your children. The healed version of yourself is one of the most profound things you can offer your children. The healed version of yourself helps you to serve your family better because you are more effective at your best. Yet all too often, we don't discipline ourselves enough to take care of ourselves. You must establish appropriate boundaries, communicate those boundaries, and take care of yourself. You must normalize getting support for what you want to achieve and for what you need. Allow yourself to receive help. Don't be so private or so prideful that you don't let someone know that there is a need in your life. Sometimes when people don't know that a need exists, they don't present information that would be helpful to you. Help them help you.

One of the things I'm working on in my personal life is getting better at recognizing that I am depleted. My husband knows that I don't like to admit when I'm tired. I think part of this is a remnant of the culture of rigorous medical education, but I think part of it is just my personality. I've always been self-critical, with high expectations and high ambitions, so being tired seems like an inconvenience more than anything. But as I've matured, I have come to appreciate the importance of taking rest, being still, and stepping back. What should be a very simple question, "Are you tired?" is often met with an attitudinal stare or an unintentionally untruthful "No." Or it may manifest with me having a mile-long to-do list, not finishing everything within the arbitrary, albeit unrealistic time frame I've set, and then feeling bad about it. As I've gotten wiser, I have been able to step back and ask myself, "What did I have to give to this project, this task, this endeavor, etc.? How can I expect to be able to do this when I have not nourished and nurtured myself properly?!" Don't worry, I'm not over here missing meals, but the point I'm making is that if I don't set myself up to be able to successfully do something, how and why should I be mad at myself when it doesn't get done?

Lastly, on the matter of self-care, I'll leave you with some sage words that my bestie, Hythia, offered me in a time of distress:

> "Sometimes American culture can make us feel like all of the things we have to do are super urgent and super necessary right now and it's the most important thing in the world. But what's most important is that you slow down, you recognize what you are feeling,

you ask for support, and you make yourself open and available to receive that support. So just to remind you, what's most important is not the work. What's most important is not what you produce. What's most important isn't even always your role. It's you. That you exist. That's valuable. This moment. That's valuable. Your wellness. That's valuable. So whenever we have to, even when it feels like a huge risk, when we have to push deadlines back, push things back to make space for ourselves and our healing, we do that. And that's valid for whatever reason."

CHAPTER 28

ON LOVE

"A bell's not a bell 'til you ring it. A song's not a song 'til you sing it. Love in your heart wasn't put there to stay. Love isn't love 'til you give it away."

—Oscar Hammerstein II

Love is a noun and a verb. Love is a feeling. Love is an act. Love is an intellectual decision to commit to fulfilling the legitimate needs of someone else. Love is consideration. Love is time. Love is paying attention. Love is protection. Love is a constant lesson. Love is many things. When the way your child wants to be loved coincides with the way that you want to love them, there is harmony. When you want your child to be satisfied with what you are comfortable giving them, even if it's not what they want or need, there is discord. The thing is, someone can love you desperately with their feelings and still not know how to love you correctly with their actions. And the truth is, we outgrow those who don't know how to love us. Love your children so they can love others and receive love. Though none of us are perfect, when we show up and when we try to love our children in the way that they need, then they receive the overflow of our willingness to get the job done. Kids want you to have a willing heart, not a perfect heart. Proceed with love.

PART III P3Q's

- What would parenting look like if it were easy?
- What do you teach your child about getting their needs met?
- How do you know love when you see it?

What do you know now that you didn't know before you read this book? Whatever it is, please have the courage to do something with it. Know that you can impact your children and your children's children. I hope you are forever changed.

Love,
Dr. Stacy

AFTERWORD

Parenting is made up of a myriad of changes. Change comes in two varieties. At one level, there can be change in the organization of your routines or other courses of action you take in your day-to-day life. The second kind of change is the end result that one person has learned something new.

In my work as a pediatrician, I realized early on that parents often were seeking the type of advice that would allow them to engage in successful actions that would result in their children managing themselves differently. Diagnoses and treatment plans aside, I realized the value in the ability to put ideas into words, to listen, to give support, to disagree reasonably, and to basically maintain a relationship with these parents in order to get to the heart of the child's well-being. As I became more skillful in my ability to carry parents through these steps, my desire to impact more families grew. I derived great joy from exploring problems with parents, developing an idea of what their expectations were, being clear in my expectations, and then getting started. There was a certain magic that transpired when I was able to come up with my own sense of both the problem and the strengths that each parent had, because all parents have strengths to offer their children, and similarly, all children have their own strengths as well. I realized that oftentimes the overwhelming part of parenthood is rooted in the inability to tease apart large amounts of hopes, fears, wants, and obligations.

In shifting some of my focus to the parents, I realized that I could facilitate positive change for the children as well, and in the process, I too have been changed. For that, I am grateful.

I give thanks and glory to God for all the ways He has given me guidance and grace. Thank you to my family. Thank you to my friends. Thank you to my ancestors. And thank you to Dr. Draion Burch (aka Dr. Drai®) and my Medical Moguls Tribe.

BIBLIOGRAPHY

Preface

Peterson, Jordan. "Society Forgot This about the Role of a Mother." YouTube, January 30, 2021. https://youtu.be/vzol6UWpkQ8.

Introduction

Howes, Lewis, and James Sexton. Marriage Secrets from a Divorce Lawyer with James Sexton. Other. *The School of Greatness Podcast*, April 11, 2018. https://lewishowes.com/podcast/marriage-secrets-from-a-divorce-lawyer-with-james-sexton/.

"The Breakfast Club." Episode. no. Phylicia Rashad On TV Motherhood, Mentoring Chadwick Boseman, HBCUs, Dynamic Acting + More. Power 105.1 FM, October 6, 2020. https://www.youtube.com/watch?v=RppgmPQnSNc.

Chapter 1

Campoamor, Danielle. "15 Things Parents Who Are Raising Tolerant Kids Do (Because It Starts With Us)." Web log. Romper (blog), June 16, 2016. https://www.romper.com/p/15-things-parents-who-are-raising-tolerant-kids-do-because-it-starts-with-us-12534.

Coleman, Patrick A. "How to Raise a Skeptical Kid Without Raising a Cynic." *Fatherly*. December 21, 2018. https://www.fatherly.com/love-money/raise-a-skeptical-not-cynical-kid-by-teaching-logic/.

"Critical Thinking: Building a Key Foundation for Language and Literacy Success." n.d. http://www.hanen.org/Helpful-Info/Early-Literacy-Corner/Critical-Thinking.aspx.

Francis, Lizzy. "How to Raise a Kid With Critical Thinking Skills (But Not an Anxious Mess)." *Fatherly*. April 26, 2019 https://www.fatherly.com/parenting/how-to-teach-kids-critical-thinking-skepticism/.

"Healing Trauma in a Toxic Culture - with Dr. Gabor Maté." Know Thyself LIVE Podcast Episode 33. YouTube, February 14, 2023. https://youtu.be/gPU0JcjybkY.

Koohi, Andrea Lynn. "More Than ABCs: Building the Critical Thinking Skills Your Child Needs for Literacy Success." Web log. *The Hanen Centre* (blog), n.d. http://www.hanen.org/Helpful-Info/ Articles/More-Than-ABCs---Building-the-Critical-Thinking-Sk. aspx.

Lakhiani, Vishen, and Dr. Shefali Tsabary. "What Is Great Parenting? Become A Better Parent." Video blog. *Mindvalley Talks* (blog), April 29, 2019. https://youtu.be/Y-OqMHxspaE.

Lee, Antoinette, and Shanti Mayers. "Episode 252. Reimagining Relationships Ft. Joél Leon." Around The Way Curls, April 6, 2023. https://podcasts.apple.com/sn/podcast/around-the-way-curls/ id1440112847.

Lythcott-Haims, Julie. "How to Raise Successful Kids -- Without Over-Parenting." TED. Lecture, October 4, 2016. https://www. youtube.com/watch?v=CyElHdaqkjo.

"Parent-Child Relationship – Why It's Important." Web log. *Parenting NI* (blog), October 25, 2018. https://www.parentingni.org/blog/ parent-child-relationship-why-its-important/.

Chapter 2

Block, Peter. *The Answer to How Is Yes: Acting on What Matters*. San Francisco, CA: Berrett-Koehler Publishers, Inc, 2003.

Coleman, Patrick A. "How to Raise a Skeptical Kid Without Raising a Cynic." *Fatherly*. December 21, 2018. https://www.fatherly.com/ love-money/raise-a-skeptical-not-cynical-kid-by-teaching-logic/.

Coleman, Patrick A. "Want a Thoughtful, Successful Child? Then Get Yourself Into Therapy." *Fatherly*. April 20, 2021. https://www. fatherly.com/parenting/parents-need-therapy/.

Demp, Barry. "'If You Are Not Willing to Learn No One Can Help You. If You Are Determined to Learn, No One Can Stop You.'" Web log. *The Quotable Coach TM* (blog). Demp Coaching & The Quotable Coach, June 19, 2018. https://www.thequotablecoach.com/if-you-are-not-willing-to-learn/.

Martin, Dr. Raquel. "Train Your Brain." Mind Your Mental Podcast, January 1, 2021. https://podcasts.apple.com/us/podcast/mind-your-mental-podcast/id1546910622.

Seales, Amanda. "Side Effects of Therapy (with Dr. Raquel Martin)." Small Doses with Amanda Seales, March 29, 2023. https://podcasts.apple.com/us/podcast/small-doses-with-amanda-seales/id1333316223.

Voge, Nic. "Self Worth Theory: The Key to Understanding & Overcoming Procrastination." TEDxPrincetonU. YouTube, December 20, 2017. https://www.youtube.com/watch?v=52lZmIafep4&t=13s.

Chapter 3

The Holy Bible: King James Version. San Diego, CA: Thunder Bay Press, 2000.

Chapter 4

Brooks, David. "The Wisdom Your Body Knows." *The New York Times*, November 28, 2019. https://www.nytimes.com/2019/11/28/opinion/brain-body-thinking.html?fbclid=IwAR01zB1N9ktQ5A-Ym4a0KaWdn-AxZjeW-r5PSEDaJaYvOXj5FsibHZ3TUBWwThe.

Delahooke, Mona. "The Hidden Cost of Planned Ignoring." Dr. Mona Delahooke - Pediatric Psychologist - California, June 15, 2015. https://monadelahooke.com/the-hidden-costs-of-planned-ignoring/.

Leo, Pam. "Connecting Through Filling the Love Cup." The Natural Child Project. Accessed April 5, 2023. https://www.naturalchild.org/articles/pam_leo/love_cup.html.

Martin, Garry, and Joseph Pear. *Behavior Modification: What It Is and How to Do It.* New York: Routledge, 2019.

McLeod, Dr. Saul. "Maslow's Hierarchy of Needs," December 29, 2020. https://www.simplypsychology.org/maslow.html.

Peer, Marisa. "World Leading Therapist: 3 Simple Steps to Remove Your Negative Thoughts." The Diary of a CEO Episode 154. YouTube, June 22, 2022. https://www.youtube.com/watch?v=bzilnhq3Mkg.

"Planned Ignoring: How to Use It to Guide Child Behaviour." Raising Children Network, October 21, 2020. https://raisingchildren.net.au/school-age/behaviour/behaviour-management-tips-tools/planned-ignoring.

"Toddlers, Meltdowns and Brain Development: Why Parents Need to Ditch Traditional Discipline." Web log. *Raised Good* (blog), n.d. https://raisedgood.com/toddlers-meltdowns-brain-development-ditch-traditional-discipline/?fbclid=IwAR2OIcYkIFhA0f6vk9oaAAvXlKMZ3ivvxh5wL7KbbrvhRXCH-qDkSL7oaSc.

Chapter 5

Carmichael, Evan. "How to TURN Your EMOTIONS Into Your SUPERPOWERS! | Brené Brown." YouTube, September 23, 2017. https://www.youtube.com/watch?v=gkWNz2G9T24&t=28s.

"Healing Trauma in a Toxic Culture - with Dr. Gabor Maté." Know Thyself LIVE Podcast Episode 33. YouTube, February 14, 2023. https://youtu.be/gPU0JcjybkY.

"Maslow's Hierarchy of Needs." How Young Children Learn, August 13, 2020. https://howyoungchildrenlearn.com/educational-foundations/maslows-hierarchy-of-needs/.

Bibliography

"Maslow's Theory of Human Needs and Child Development." Pro-Solutions Training. Accessed May 14, 2021. https://www.prosolutionstraining.com/resources/articles/maslows-theory-of-human-needs-and-child-development.cfm.

McLeod, Dr. Saul. "Maslow's Hierarchy of Needs," December 29, 2020. https://www.simplypsychology.org/maslow.html.

Williams, David. "Child Development Theories: Abraham Maslow." First Discoverers, August 17, 2020. https://www.firstdiscoverers.co.uk/abraham-maslow-child-development-theories.

Chapter 6

Colaianni, Paul. "Podcast: Can Dysfunctions Be Useful?" The Overwhelmed Brain, July 18, 2021.https://theoverwhelmedbrain.com/podcasts?ppplayer=b7a2020a250fe88086a4b3754451875b&ppepisode=573a10fbbfbbfafbf9440a5bebed8021.

Chapter 7

Goldowitz, Dr. Dan, and Dr. Pat Levitt. Why Early Matters for Healthy Brain and Child Development. Other. *The Urban Child Institute,* April 4, 2016. http://www.urbanchildinstitute.org/resources/videos/why-early-matters-for-healthy-brain-and-child-development.

"Healing Trauma in a Toxic Culture - with Dr. Gabor Maté." Know Thyself LIVE Podcast Episode 33. YouTube, February 14, 2023. https://youtu.be/gPU0JcjybkY.

Moore, Wes. "Wes Moore: The Difference Between Your Job and Your Work | SuperSoul Sessions | OWN." YouTube. YouTube, May 10, 2017. https://www.youtube.com/watch?v=64O1T8rvC9I.

"Understanding the Effects of Maltreatment on Brain Development." Child Welfare Information Gateway. Children's Bureau, April 2015. https://www.childwelfare.gov/pubPDFs/brain_development.pdf.

Chapter 8

Runkle, Anna. "Limerence: Abandonment Wounds Cue Partners to Discard You." Crappy Childhood Fairy. YouTube, January 25, 2022. https://www.youtube.com/watch?v=8VAR0Yt6H5c.

Chapter 9

"A Call to Men." A Call to Men – The next generation of manhood. Accessed July 2021. https://www.acalltomen.org/.

Cook, Dr. Bethany. "Raising Boys Without Perpetuating Toxic Masculinity." Mabelandmoxie. Mabel + Moxie, May 11, 2020. https://www.mabelandmoxie.com/Raising+Boys+Without+Perpetuating+Toxic+Masculinity.

Mooney, Taylor. "Is There a Better Way to Raise Boys to Avoid Toxic Masculinity?" CBS News. CBS Interactive, December 5, 2019. https://www.cbsnews.com/news/raising-boys-toxic-masculinity-cbsn-documentary/.

Peer, Marisa. "World Leading Therapist: 3 Simple Steps to Remove Your Negative Thoughts." The Diary of a CEO Episode 154. YouTube, June 22, 2022. https://www.youtube.com/watch?v=bzilnhq3Mkg.

Chapter 11

"7 Ways to Protect Kids From Sexual Abuse | AAP." American Academy of Pediatrics. YouTube, March 31, 2023. https://www.youtube.com/watch?v=ACvqz9Ws9-w.

"Child Abuse Expert Installed as Inaugural Washington Children's Foundation Professor of Child and Adolescent Protection." Children's National Hospital. Accessed May 14, 2021. https://childrensnational.org/en/news-and-events/childrens-newsroom/2017/child-expert-installed-as-inaugural-childrens-foundation-professor-child-and-adolescent-protection.

Nienow, Dr. Shalon. "Seven Steps to Teaching Children Body Autonomy." Rady Children's Hospital-San Diego. Rady Children's Hospital-San Diego. Accessed May 15, 2021. https://www.rchsd.org/2019/12/seven-steps-to-teaching-children-body-autonomy/.

Sands, Nicole. "Months before Interviewing Michael Jackson Accusers, Oprah Winfrey Opened up about Her Own Abuse." PEOPLE.com, March 5, 2019. https://people.com/tv/oprah-winfrey-details-own-abuse-months-before-interviewing-michael-jackson-accusers/.

Chapter 12

Kale, Neha, and Isabella Moore. "Women and Ageing: 'I've Developed the Courage to Live My Own Truth' – Picture Essay." The Guardian. Guardian News and Media, December 29, 2018. https://www.theguardian.com/lifeandstyle/2018/dec/30/women-and-ageing-ive-developed-the-courage-to-live-my-own-truth-picture-essay.

Kaye, Deirdre. "These 55 Quotes About Growing Up Are Totally Sweet (And 100% Relatable)." Scary Mommy, September 22, 2021. https://www.scarymommy.com/growing-up-quotes/.

Chapter 13

"What Is Sexual Consent?: Facts About Rape & Sexual Assault." Planned Parenthood. Accessed May 13, 2021. https://www.plannedparenthood.org/learn/relationships/sexual-consent.

Chapter 14

Howes, Lewis, and Bob Proctor. "The 7 Things Poor People Do That the RICH DON'T! | Lewis Howes." YouTube. YouTube, October 12, 2020. https://www.youtube.com/watch?v=Kc-5BQXN3A&t=31s.

Proctor, Bob. *You Were Born Rich: Now You Can Discover and Develop Those Riches*. Scottsdale, AZ: Proctor Gallagher Institute, 2014.

Chapter 15

Dubois, Lise, Maikol Diasparra, Brigitte Bédard, Jaakko Kaprio, Bénédicte Fontaine-Bisson, Richard Tremblay, Michel Boivin, and Daniel Pérusse. "Genetic and Environmental Influences on Eating Behaviors in 2.5- AND 9-Year-Old Children: A Longitudinal Twin Study." *International Journal of Behavioral Nutrition and Physical Activity* 10, no. 1 (2013): 134. https://doi.org/10.1186/1479-5868-10-134.

Grimm, Eleanor R, and Nanette I Steinle. "Genetics of Eating Behavior: Established and Emerging Concepts." *Nutrition Reviews* 69, no. 1 (2011): 52–60. https://doi.org/10.1111/j.1753-4887.2010.00361.x.

"In Baby's 'First Bite,' a Chance to Shape a Child's Taste." NPR. NPR, February 4, 2016. https://www.npr.org/sections/thesalt/2016/02/04/465305656/in-babys-first-bite-a-chance-to-shape-a-childs-taste.

Scaglioni, Silvia, Chiara Arrizza, Fiammetta Vecchi, and Sabrina Tedeschi. "Determinants of Children's Eating Behavior." *The American Journal of Clinical Nutrition* 94, no. suppl_6 (2011). https://doi.org/10.3945/ajcn.110.001685.

Chapter 16

"What It Means to Be a Mother." Web log. *Exploring Your Mind* (blog), November 21, 2015. https://exploringyourmind.com/what-it-means-to-be-a-mother/.

Chapter 17

Block, Peter. *Flawless Consulting: A Guide to Getting Your Expertise Used*. 3rd ed. Hoboken, NJ: Pfeiffer, 2011.

Chapter 18

Roberts, Robin, and Tabitha Brown. "Tabitha Brown Dishes on New Book, 'Feeding the Soul.'" Good Morning America, September 29, 2021. https://www.goodmorningamerica.com/culture/video/tabitha-brown-dishes-book-feeding-soul-80298443.

Vegvary, Lisa. "Role of Grandparents in Modern Families." North State Parent Magazine, October 30, 2019. https://northstateparent.com/article/include-grandparents-modern-family/.

Chapter 19

"How Not to Take Things Personally? | Frederik Imbo | TEDxMechelen." YouTube. TEDxTalks, March 4, 2020. https://www.youtube.com/watch?v=LnJwH_PZXnM.

"My Intense First Therapy Session with My Mom." YouTube. Hello Hunnay with Jeannie Mai, March 11, 2021. https://www.youtube.com/watch?v=_LCYTbYdIXU.

Chapter 20

"An Open Letter to All Black Men." Episode. *Iyanla Fix My Life 8*, no. 6. OWN, May 15, 2021.

Coleman, Patrick A. "Want a Thoughtful, Successful Child? Then Get Yourself Into Therapy." *Fatherly*. April 20, 2021. https://www.fatherly.com/parenting/parents-need-therapy/.

Lowenstein, Dr. Dave. "What's Your Discipline Style?" Dr. David Lowenstein and Associates, March 6, 2013. https://www.drlowenstein.com/2013/03/06/whats-your-discipline-style/.

Maté, Dr. Gabor. "How Not to Screw Up Your Kids." London Real. YouTube, December 22, 2018. https://www.youtube.com/watch?v=gX4EFwv76Vg.

Peterson, Dr. Jordan B, and Lewis Howes. "THIS IS Why Most People Are LAZY & UNMOTIVATED IN LIFE!" YouTube. YouTube, April 12, 2021. https://www.youtube.com/watch?v=ylTHKT4HSBc&t=4017s.

Siegel, Daniel J., and Tina Payne Bryson. *No-Drama Discipline: The Whole-Brain Way to Calm the Chaos and Nurture Your Child's Developing Mind.* New York: Bantam Books, an imprint of Random House, a division of Penguin Random House LLC, 2016.

Tsabary, Shefali. *Out of Control: Why Disciplining Your Child Doesn't Work - and What Will.* Philadelphia, USA: Running Press, 2014.

Chapter 21

Christensen, Deborah. "Primary and Secondary Emotions." Corner Canyon Counseling, 2015. https://cornercanyoncounseling.com/wp-content/uploads/2015/05/Primary-and-Secondary-Emotions.pdf.

Greenberg, Leslie S. "Emotion-Focused Therapy: A Clinical Synthesis." FOCUS, January 1, 2010. https://focus.psychiatryonline.org/doi/10.1176/foc.8.1.foc32.

Khan, Nadia. "What Are Primary And Secondary Emotions." Betterhelp. BetterHelp, February 11, 2018. https://www.betterhelp.com/advice/general/what-are-primary-and-secondary-emotions/.

Kolk, Bessel van der. *The Body Keeps the Score: Brain, Mind, and Body in the Healing of Trauma.* London: Penguin Books, 2015.

Mollick, Lynn. "Leslie Greenberg's Master Lecture on Emotion-Focused Therapy." NJ-ACT. Accessed May 16, 2021. https://nj-act.org/greenberg.html.

Tull, Matthew. "How Primary Emotions Affect You." Edited by Akeem Marsh. Verywell Mind, March 21, 2021. https://www.verywellmind.com/primary-emotions-2797378.

Chapter 22

Hornor, Gail. "Attachment Disorders." *Journal of Pediatric Health Care* 33, no. 5 (2019): 612–22. https://doi.org/10.1016/j.pedhc.2019. 04.017.

Li, Pamela. "How to Deal with Externalizing Behavior in Children." Parenting For Brain, April 9, 2023. https://www.parentingforbrain. com/externalizing-behavior/.

Li, Pamela. "Internalizing Behavior in Children - Examples and Risk Factors." Parenting For Brain, April 6, 2023. https://www.parentingforbrain.com/internalizing-behavior/.

Liu, Jianghong. "Childhood Externalizing Behavior: Theory and Implications." *Journal of Child and Adolescent Psychiatric Nursing* 17, no. 3 (2004): 93–103. https://doi.org/10.1111/j.1744-6171.2004.tb000 03.x.

Parenting, and BabySparks. "Infant-Parent Attachment: The Four Types & Why They Matter." BabySparks, June 18, 2019. https:// babysparks.com/2019/06/18/infant-parent-attachment-the-four-types-why-they-matter/.

"Parent-Child Relationship - Why It's Important." Parenting NI, October 25, 2018. https://www.parentingni.org/blog/parent-child-relationship-why-its-important/.

Slade, Arietta, and Jeremy Holmes. "Attachment and Psychotherapy." *Current Opinion in Psychology* 25 (2019): 152–56. https://doi. org/10.1016/j.copsyc.2018.06.008.

Teahan, Patrick. "Do You Navigate People? 4 Examples - Codependency and Trauma." Patrick Teahan LICSW. YouTube, August 17, 2022. https://www.youtube.com/watch?v=qyxSX6gH-jY.

"The 4 Attachment Styles and How They Impact You." Cleveland Clinic, September 23, 2022. https://health.clevelandclinic.org/ attachment-theory-and-attachment-styles/.

Thompson, Ross, R. Biswas-Diener, and Ed Diener. "Social and Personality Development in Childhood." Essay. In *Noba Textbook Series: Psychology*. Champaign, IL: DEF publishers, 2021.

Chapter 23

Bain, David Gordon. "Trauma Theory, Attachment-Detachment Theory, Defensive-Fantasy Theory, and How Freud Got the Oedipal Complex Partly Wrong." *Journal of Hospital & Medical Management*, 17, 3, no. 2 (October 25, 2017). https://doi.org/https://hospital-medical-management.imedpub.com/trauma-theory-attachmentdetachment-theory-defensivefantasy-theory-and-how-freud-got-the-oedipal-complex-partly-wrong.php?aid=20682.

Durham, Saranne. "What Is Reconciliation?" The South African College of Applied Psychology - SACAP, December 17, 2021. https://www.sacap.edu.za/blog/applied-psychology/what is reconciliation/#:~:text=Reconciliation%20is%20a%20psychological%20process,mental%2C%20emotional%20and%20physical%20healing.

Shrivastava, Anshu. "Parent-Children's Relationship: Aren't Children Responsible for Maintaining It?" Web log. *Anshushrivastava.com* (blog). anshushrivastava.com, n.d. https://anshushrivastava.com/parenting-tips/parent-childrens-relationship-arent-children-responsible-for-maintaining-it/.

Stein, Joshua David. "Love Isn't Math. It's Bigger Than That." *Fatherly*. April 29, 2019. https://www.fatherly.com/love-money/joshua-david-stein-letters-to-boys-about-love/.

"Vision of Marriage: Cheers to Closure." Episode. *Put a Ring On It* 2, no. 207. OWN, August 6, 2021.

Chapter 24

Behrman, Richard E., and Marilyn J. Field, eds. "Appendix E - Bereavement Experiences After The Death Of A Child." Essay. In *WHEN CHILDREN DIE: Improving Palliative and End-of-Life Care for Children and Their Families*. Washington, D.C.: National Academy Press, 2003. https://www.ncbi.nlm.nih.gov/books/NBK220798/.

"Guidelines for Health Supervision of Infants, Children, and Adolescents: Promoting Safety and Injury Prevention." Bright Futures. American Academy of Pediatrics, n.d. https://brightfutures.aap.org/Bright%20Futures%20Documents/BF4_Safety.pdf.

"The Grief of Parents When a Child Dies." The Compassionate Friends: Supporting Family After A Child Dies, October 5, 2018. https://www.compassionatefriends.org/grief/.

Chapter 25

Hogenboom, Melissa. "The Hidden Load: How 'Thinking of Everything' Holds Mums Back." BBC Worklife. BBC, May 18, 2021. https://www.bbc.com/worklife/article/20210518-the-hidden-load-how-thinking-of-everything-holds-mums-back.

Lockman, Darcy. "Where Do Kids Learn to Undervalue Women? From Their Parents." The Washington Post. WP Company, November 10, 2017. https://www.washingtonpost.com/outlook/where-do-kids-learn-to-undervalue-women-from-their-parents/2017/11/10/724518b2-c439-11e7-afe9-4f60b5a6c4a0_story.html.

Moyer, Melinda Wenner. "Kids Learn Sexism Very Early. Here's How Parents Can Help Them Unlearn It." Slate Magazine. Slate, November 6, 2017. https://slate.com/human-interest/2017/11/how-to-stop-sexism-and-raise-a-son-who-respects-women.html.

Sole-Smith, Virginia. "How to Share the Parenting Load with Your Partner." Parents. Parents, August 20, 2018. https://www.

parents.com/parenting/better-parenting/advice/ways-to-share-the-parenting-load-with-your-partner/.

TedX Talks. "4 Habits of ALL Successful Relationships | Dr. Andrea & Jonathan Taylor-Cummings | TEDxSquareMile." YouTube. TEDx Talks, June 21, 2019. https://youtu.be/o4Y5Mr8rZ9A.

Chapter 26

Bingham-Smith, Katie. "There's No Love Like the Love Your Kids Have For You When They Are Small." Mom, April 19, 2017. https://mom.com/toddler/63729-there-no-love-love-your-kids-have-when-they-are-small/i-also-know-women-who-have-been-there?utm_content=beingamom_fanpage&utm_source=cafe&utm_medium=Facebook&fbclid=IwAR26woK9Wfd-vQb58irXVAthzC0E1PeW_f5r_B4esWS9ZdZANnDL-ldmnxks.

Jordan, Andy. "Is Multi-Tasking a Bad Thing?" Project Management Institute, September 8, 2021. https://www.projectmanagement.com/articles/727103/Is-Multi-Tasking-a-Bad-Thing-.

Schlicher, Erin. "Parental Burnout - 4 Tips to Combat Parental Fatigue." Empowering Parents, June 1, 2021. https://www.empoweringparents.com/article/im-so-exhausted-4-tips-to-combat-parental-burnout/.

Chapter 27

Ejpseaks. "You Know You Need It!" YouTube. Ejspeaks, January 13, 2017. https://www.youtube.com/watch?v=Xn_YymcnN4U.

The Same Room. "Jeannie Mai Jenkins Talks Journeying to Wholeness, Self Love, and the Power of Healthy Environments." YouTube. The Same Room, October 20, 2021. https://youtu.be/tmfRawAfzEY.

Chapter 28

"Unanswered Questions." Episode. *Married at First Sight* 12, no. 13. Lifetime, April 7, 2021.

ABOUT THE AUTHOR

Dr. Stacy Cary-Thompson is a clinician, consultant, and parenting coach. Passionate about child advocacy, she goes beyond her role as a pediatrician to provide hard-earned insights and expert advice to parents and guardians so that every child in her care has the opportunity to be raised in a healthy, responsive household.

She is also the founder and CEO of *Cary Cares Parenting LLC*, where she offers parents an extended village as they navigate their parenthood journey. She aims to transform lives for generations by encouraging parents and parent-proxies to be knowledgeable, responsive, and reflective. Through her online program, she works with parents one-on-one to help them understand their children's behavior, navigate various stages of development, and form authentic connections with their children. Additionally, she speaks to companies and brands to advance conversation about the complexities of being a parent and also a member of the workforce.

Dr. Cary-Thompson graduated from Lafayette College with a bachelor of science in neuroscience in 2007, and in 2014, she received her medical degree from Howard University College of Medicine. She then completed her pediatric residency at the Children's Hospital of Georgia in Augusta. She now resides in Washington, D.C. with her husband and son.

Learn more at
www.drstacymd.com

Printed in the USA
CPSIA information can be obtained
at www.ICGtesting.com
LVHW020410190923
758520LV00031B/222

9 781644 844953